The Complete Guide to

Currency Trading & Investing

*How to Earn High Rates of
Return Safely and Take Control
of Your Financial Investments*

REVISED 2ND EDITION

By Martha Maeda and Jamaine Burrell

The Complete Guide to Currency Trading & Investing: How to Earn High Rates of Return Safely and Take Control of Your Financial Investments REVISED 2ND EDITION

Copyright © 2011 Atlantic Publishing Group, Inc.
1405 SW 6th Avenue • Ocala, Florida 34471 • Phone 800-814-1132 • Fax 352-622-1875
Web site: www.atlantic-pub.com • E-mail: sales@atlantic-pub.com
SAN Number: 268-1250

Burrell, Jamaine, 1958-
  The complete guide to currency trading & investing : how to earn high rates of return safely and take control of your financial investments / by Jamaine Burrell and Martha Maeda. -- Rev. 2nd ed.
    p. cm.
  Includes bibliographical references and index.
  ISBN-13: 978-1-60138-442-3 (alk. paper)
  ISBN-10: 1-60138-442-4 (alk. paper)
  1. Foreign exchange market. 2. Foreign exchange futures. I. Maeda, Martha, 1953- II. Title.
  HG3851.B87 2011
  332.4'5--dc22
                        2010028232

Printed in the United States

PROJECT MANAGER: Melissa Peterson • mpeterson@atlantic-pub.com
PROOFREADER: Katy Doll • ASSISTANT EDITOR: Brad Goldbach
INTERIOR DESIGN: James Ryan Hamilton • james@jamesryanhamilton.com
COVER DESIGNS: Jackie Miller • millerjackiej@gmail.com

Printed on Recycled Paper

We recently lost our beloved pet "Bear," who was not only our best and dearest friend but also the "Vice President of Sunshine" here at Atlantic Publishing. He did not receive a salary but worked tirelessly 24 hours a day to please his parents. Bear was a rescue dog that turned around and showered myself, my wife Sherri, his grandparents Jean, Bob and Nancy and every person and animal he met (maybe not rabbits) with friendship and love. He made a lot of people smile every day.

We wanted you to know that a portion of the profits of this book will be donated to The Humane Society of the United States. *–Douglas & Sherri Brown*

The human-animal bond is as old as human history. We cherish our animal companions for their unconditional affection and acceptance. We feel a thrill when we glimpse wild creatures in their natural habitat or in our own backyard.

Unfortunately, the human-animal bond has at times been weakened. Humans have exploited some animal species to the point of extinction.

The Humane Society of the United States makes a difference in the lives of animals here at home and worldwide. The HSUS is dedicated to creating a world where our relationship with animals is guided by compassion. We seek a truly humane society in which animals are respected for their intrinsic value, and where the human-animal bond is strong.

Want to help animals? We have plenty of suggestions. Adopt a pet from a local shelter, join The Humane Society and be a part of our work to help companion animals and wildlife. You will be funding our educational, legislative, investigative and outreach projects in the U.S. and across the globe.

Or perhaps you'd like to make a memorial donation in honor of a pet, friend or relative? You can through our Kindred Spirits program. And if you'd like to contribute in a more structured way, our Planned Giving Office has suggestions about estate planning, annuities, and even gifts of stock that avoid capital gains taxes.

Maybe you have land that you would like to preserve as a lasting habitat for wildlife. Our Wildlife Land Trust can help you. Perhaps the land you want to share is a backyard—that's enough. Our Urban Wildlife Sanctuary Program will show you how to create a habitat for your wild neighbors.

So you see, it's easy to help animals. And The HSUS is here to help.

2100 L Street NW • Washington, DC 20037 • 202-452-1100
www.hsus.org

SWITZERLAND
CANADA
USTRALIA
WEEDEN
NMARK
WAY
0.7708
1.5279
1.8295
1.7999
9.3450
7.5750
8.0146
00.000

Table of Contents

Chapter 4: The Language of Forex 89

Chapter 5: Fundamental Analysis 105

Foreword

Portfolio management theory is simple financial economics: A diversified portfolio of uncorrelated asset classes can provide the highest returns with the least amount of risk.

Serious investors know they must diversify their portfolio. Most will turn to stocks, bonds, or real estate — all fine choices, but one must consciously seek out assets that do not move lockstep with each other. By its very nature currency trading is inflation proof, as it is not tied directly to the world's stock market. A currency trading portfolio will likely benefit despite conventional market fluctuations.

The art of currency trading is a sea of opportunity to the well informed. Being educated in how these markets work and how to use today's tools can transform you into a successful investor while actually reducing your overall risk. Information to navigate the liquid, easy-to-trade forex or futures markets is abundantly available on the Internet in a plethora of trading platforms.

When I began investing in currency trading almost 20 years ago, we learned the basics by trial and error — and we made many mistakes! Even today, too few publications provide basic information for novice traders. *The Complete Guide to Currency Trading & Investing* is now one of those few publications. Starting with this book, you can become a confident trader. Of course, any new form of investment strategy will take a serious commitment, but you will be greatly rewarded.

Mark L. Waggoner
President, Excel Futures, Inc.
16691 Gothard Street, Suite #L
Huntington Beach, CA. 92647
www.excelfutures.com
Toll Free: (888) 959-9955
International: 01-714-843-9884

Mark Waggoner is the president of Excel Futures in Huntington Beach, California and has been trading since 1990. He publishes a daily and weekly trade advisory: "The Trade Accord" and "The TrendTracker" respectively. Waggoner is frequently a guest on Bloomberg Television and Radio and provides market commentary to Reuters and CNBC.

Introduction

C urrency trading, also known as forex, FX, and foreign exchange, attracted increasing attention from individual investors after they watched the U.S. stock market lose 43 percent of its value in 2008. Currency trading, which has little correlation with the stock market, is essentially speculation that the currency of a particular country is going to rise or fall in value against the currency of another country. There is always a winning side in a currency trade because, as the value of one currency falls, the relative value of the other rises. If you have the knowledge and the foresight to be on the winning side, you will make a profit from your trade.

Several aspects of currency trading appeal to active investors. The global foreign exchange market is the largest and one of the most liquid financial markets in the world. A recent survey of the Bank for International Settlements (BIS), carried out in April 2007, estimated that the global daily average turnover in traditional foreign exchange instruments was $3.2 trillion — or nearly $500 a day for every man, woman, and child on earth. About $1 trillion of this was the type of "spot" foreign exchange trades that individual currency exchange traders are mostly involved in. The currency trading market is not centralized in a single exchange or location — it is an over-the-counter (OTC) market, meaning it consists of millions of individual trades taking place among banks, brokers, and dealers at various currency trading locations around the world. This makes the currency market very fluid because individual, large traders cannot manipulate prices, as is done in the stock market. All currencies can be traded electronically 24 hours a day, almost six days a week. Sales of a nation's currency do not stop at the close of that nation's business day. As markets are closing in one part of the world, they are becoming active in another part of the world, keeping price movements steady and eliminating gaps between the time that a sale is initiated and the time it is concluded.

Until the late 1990s, currency trading was conducted mostly by financial institutions and large corporations, because private investors had little access to pricing information and could not trade efficiently. The growth of the Internet changed everything, and in 1997, the first foreign currency trading platform opened on the Internet, offering individuals the opportunity to actively invest in currency trades. Now, with as little as $200, you can open a currency trading account with one of the numerous online forex firms that provide systems for placing orders, called trading platforms, along with live price charts, news and information, education, and customer service. Many of these firms allow you to multiply your profits by trading on margin (an arrangement in which the firm loans you money to use for trading), and break currency trades into mini lots and micro lots, so that you can participate even with a small investment.

Currency trading is a speculative investment that involves taking calculated financial risks in an effort to realize a profit. You cannot succeed by trading based on instinct or "gut feeling." Currency trading requires commitment, time, and effort. A successful currency trader does extensive research and knows his or her market thoroughly. Experienced currency traders emphasize the importance of emotional and financial self-discipline, perseverance, and decisiveness. No one can win consistently. Every currency trader suffers losses. Successful currency trading depends on developing a personal trading strategy and establishing strict boundaries to manage risk and limit losses. Over time, your profits will outweigh your losses.

Currency traders make decisions using a combination of two types of analysis: technical and fundamental. Fundamental analysis is the study of global and national economic, political, and social factors that affect that value of a currency. Historically, certain events, such as the release of economic news in a specific country, have a demonstrated effect on currency values, at least temporarily. A knowledgeable trader anticipates such events and profits from price fluctuations. Technical analysis is the observation of patterns in price behavior using past pricing information displayed on charts and graphs. Certain visual patterns in a graph or chart typically precede a rise or fall in the value of a currency and can be used to determine when to buy or sell. Over time, traders learn to combine these patterns with other information to predict a profitable trade.

Most online forex brokers allow you to practice with a "demo" or "paper" account before you begin trading with real money. Demo accounts allow you to familiarize yourself with a trading platform before you commit to a particular broker. Try currency trading with a demo account to get a feeling for price fluctuations and develop your trading strategy before jumping into the market. When you are able to realize a consistent profit with a demo account, you are ready to begin trading with real money.

This book is an introduction to currency trading. Each chapter covers an important topic, such as the nature of the currency market, central banks and government agencies that influence monetary policy, the effect of political and social events on currency prices, fundamental and technical analysis, and risk management. Readers will learn how to select a broker and a trading platform and how to begin trading for themselves.

Throughout the book, important points highlighted as "tips" and "case studies" give insight and advice from experienced traders. Many forex terms are expressed as acronyms; each term is spelled out the first time it is used in the book. *You will find a list of acronyms in Appendix A. A glossary of common forex terms can be found at the end of the book, and a list of resources and websites to further your education and research is included in Appendix F.*

After reading this book, you may decide currency trading is not for you, but that you would still like exposure to the currency market in your portfolio. If this is the case, the last chapter explains how you can participate in forex by investing through a commodity trading adviser or by buying shares of a currency exchange-traded fun (ETF) or mutual fund.

Learning about currency trading will not only open your eyes to an exciting and active trading opportunity; it will help you understand the forces that move our global economy.

TIP: Trade only with money that you can afford to lose.

Currency trading can be very profitable, but it also involves considerable risk, especially for a novice. Trade only with money that you can afford to lose and manage risk by setting stop limits. *See Chapter 7 for information on risk management.*

Chapter 1

What is Currency Trading?

Currency trading is the simultaneous buying and selling of national currencies on the foreign exchange market (forex). The forex market is the largest financial trade market in the world, with an estimated trading volume of more than $3 trillion per day, triple the volume of the stock markets and other futures markets combined. This figure includes derivative currency trading tools, such as futures, forwards, options, and swaps, as well as the spot trading that is most commonly used in forex.

Spot refers to the price at which you can buy or sell a currency at this exact moment. The spot market is most commonly used in forex because spot trading allows financial instruments to be traded at the current market price. Spot transactions are typically settled within two business days, in contrast to futures, forwards, options, and swaps, which are contracts to trade financial instruments at some time in the future. More than 40 percent of all forex trades are settled within two days, and 80 percent of all forex trades are settled within two weeks. Unlike other types of financial markets, the forex spot market has no central physical location for exchange. It is a strictly electronic trading process revolving around a network of individuals, corporations, and banks. The forex market operates uninterrupted 24 hours a day, almost six days a week (based on time zones), as long as dealers are open for business in some part of the world.

Currency trades are always executed in pairs: One currency is bought while the other is simultaneously sold. Forex traders make money by buying a currency when they anticipate its value is going to rise against the value of the currency being sold. If the value does go up, the trader then locks in a profit by selling that currency. In order to understand forex trading, it is necessary to understand the nature of the foreign exchange market and the major forces and economic factors that influence currency values.

Physical currency rarely changes hands in forex transactions. Each purchase or sale represents an actual amount of a national currency held in a deposit in one of that nation's banks or in the foreign currency reserves of a bank in another country. Because the supply of a particular currency is finite, prices go up when that currency is in demand and down when everyone is trying to sell it.

The Forex Market and the Stock Market

Forex trading resembles stock trading, with some important differences. Most currency trades are executed within a very short time period of a few minutes, hours, or days to take advantage of temporary fluctuations in market prices. Ownership of stock represents ownership of interest in a company or business. Active stock traders may try to profit from market fluctuations by buying and selling shares of stock within short time periods, but stocks can also be bought and held for decades while they increase in value. Currency typically does not steadily increase in value over time — it is range-bound, meaning that over time prices rise and fall within certain upper and lower boundaries.

U.S. stocks can only be bought and sold during U.S. business hours, when the stock exchanges are open. Stock prices can change significantly between the close of the market on one day and its opening the next morning — a time gap that can cause delays in executing orders or prevent a trader from locking in profits. A forex trader can trade whenever prices are favorable. Part-time forex traders can develop a trading strategy suited to a specific time period every day. For example, a person could trade forex between 7 p.m. and 9 p.m. each evening, using a currency pair that is actively trading during that period.

Stocks sometimes experience problems with liquidity, such as when demand outstrips supply or too many sellers enter the market at once, making it difficult to find buyers. The forex market is highly liquid, with a daily trading volume of approximately $3.2 trillion in currency instruments, including $1 trillion in spot trades.

The profit on each unit of currency in a trade is typically very small — a fraction of a cent. Therefore, currency must be traded in large volumes in order to realize a reasonable profit. Forex brokers allow traders leverage of anywhere from 50:1 to 400:1, greatly increasing the potential profit (or loss) from a trade. You can begin forex trading with only a small investment of $250 and control $12,500 in currency by leveraging your investment at a 50:1 ratio. Stockbrokers require a minimum of at least $2,000 to open an investment account and charge interest for leverage.

A novice currency trader only needs to be familiar with the basic characteristics of four or five major currencies. In contrast, to actively invest in stocks, an investor must research each individual company, its financial condition, and its status relative to other companies in the same industry and market sector, as well as national and global economic trends.

Comparison: Trading Forex and Trading Stocks

	Forex	U.S. Stocks
Liquidity	Highly liquid 24 hours a day, 5.5 days a week	Highly liquid while the stock exchanges are open
Leverage	50:1 to 400:1	Up to 50% of your equity
Trading hours	24 hours a day, 2:00 pm Sunday - 5:00 pm Friday EST	9:00 am to 4:00 pm EST, Monday - Friday
Broker commissions and fees	Dealers profit from the spread. An electronic communication network (ECN) may charge commissions on trades	Brokers receive commissions on trades
Short selling	Unlimited short selling	Restrictions on short selling and stop orders
Number of products	Knowledge of 5 major currencies is enough	More than 8,000 stocks
Exchange	OTC market, no formal currency exchange	Each stock sells on the exchange where it is listed
Security	Major currencies will not fail; A loss is irrevocable when a trade is settled	Even a well-known corporation can fail without prior notice; When stock prices drop, investors still hold an interest in the company and the price may rise again

Currencies

Currency trading can involve any currency backed by an existing nation. The greatest volume of forex trading involves the currencies of the world's largest economies, known as major currencies. Currencies that are less heavily traded are called exotics. *For more information on currencies used in forex trading, see Appendix C.*

Major currencies

The seven currencies listed in the table below represent the major forex currency markets and are used in those nations with the highest trading volume; all other currencies are considered minor. Until recently, the U.S. dollar dominated the global economy, but the euro has emerged as a strong and stable contender. Almost all foreign banks hold large reserves of U.S. dollars as security, and one of the most crucial commodities in the world, oil, is paid for in U.S. dollars.

Each currency is represented by a three-letter symbol. In most currencies, the first two letters symbolize the nation, and the last letter symbolizes the name of currency.

Seven Major Currency Markets

Symbol	Currency	Nation
USD	Dollar	United States of America
EUR	Euro	Members of Economic and Monetary Union
JPY	Yen	Japan
GBP	Pound	Great Britain
CHF	Franc	Switzerland (Confederation Helvetica)
CAD	Dollar	Canada
AUD	Dollar	Australia

The euro is an exception to the three-letter symbolism. Eleven European nations agreed in 1999 to remove their existing currencies from circulation and replace them with the euro. On Jan. 1, 2002, the euro became the official currency of these nations and of a twelfth nation — Greece. These 12 nations are known as the Economic and Monetary Union (EMU). The following table notes the different members:

Twelve Nations of the Economic and Monetary Union (EMU)

Nation	Old Currency	Old Symbol	New Symbol
Austria	Schilling	ATS	EUR
Belgium	Franc	BEF	EUR
Finland	Markka	FIM	EUR
France	Franc	FRF	EUR

Germany	Deutsche Mark	DEM	EUR
Greece	Drachma	GRD	EUR
Ireland	Punt	IEP	EUR
Italy	Lira	ITL	EUR
Luxemburg	Franc	LUF	EUR
The Netherlands	Guilder	NLG	EUR
Portugal	Escudo	PTE	EUR
Spain	Peseta	ESP	EUR

In addition, the new currency was adopted by:

- The Vatican City

- The Principality of Andorra

- The Principality of Monaco

- The Republic of San Marion

- Any place that previously used one or more of the currencies that were used in the 12 euro nations, as well as any territories, departments, collections, or possessions of those 12 European nations, including:

Europa Island	Martinique	Saint Pierre
French Guiana	Mayotte	The Azores
Guadeloupe	Miquelon	The Balearic Islands
Juan de Nova	Réunion	The Canary Islands
The Madeira Islands	Saint Martin	

The euro is the currency of some of the wealthiest nations in the world. Used by more than 300 million people, it is considered a rival to the U.S. dollar. Many people expect that the euro will replace the U.S. dollar as the currency kept in reserve by the world.

The four most actively traded currency pairs are EUR/USD (euro against U.S. dollar), USD/JPY (U.S. dollar against Japanese yen), GBP/USD (British pound against U.S. dollar), and USD/CHF (U.S. dollar against Swiss franc). The EUR/USD pair is considered the most actively traded financial instrument in the world. Though not included in the "majors," AUD/USD (Australian dollar against U.S. dollar) and USD/CAD (U.S. dollar against Canadian dollar) are also heavily traded.

The G8

Another important group of nations in the currency market is the G8, a group of eight of the world's richest economies. The members of G8 are:

G8 Member Nations

Nation	Currency	Country Code
U.S.	Dollar	USD
Great Britain	Pound	GBP
Canada	Dollar	CAD
France	Euro	EUR
Germany	Euro	EUR
Italy	Euro	EUR
Japan	Yen	JPY
Russia	Ruble	RUB

Leaders of the G8 nations meet at least once a year. Though many regard these gatherings as little more than photo opportunities for heads of state, the meetings influence currency levels and provide insight into the global economic mood. Whether a nation is prospering or struggling economically, its leaders discuss its growth and current needs at these meetings.

Exotics

Currencies of lesser-known countries are known as exotics. These currencies offer good trading opportunities but require research and a clear understanding of the economic and political circumstances of the country. Actively traded exotics tend to be safer and offer tighter spreads, more precise price execution, and more transparent price disclosure than other exotics. The most actively traded exotics include the New Zealand dollar (NZD), the South African rand (ZAR), and the Singapore dollar (SGD). Other significant exotics include the Chinese yuan (CNY), Brazilian real (BRR), and South Korean won (KRW).

The Chinese yuan (or renminbi) is linked to the U.S. dollar, but the Chinese government does not allow its currency to float freely, as the United States and most other industrialized nations do. *See Chapter 3 for more information on this topic.* Because of the size of the Chinese economy, it is expected that if the Chinese government does release hold of its currency, the yuan will become one of the major world currencies. This is a major topic for journalists and commentators, but no one is sure if or when this will happen. The South African rand floats against other world currencies and is a major secondary currency in the market. The Brazilian real is only open to offshore counterparties but has floated since it was devalued in 1999. The South Korean won plays a major role in Asian economic prosperity but is not easy to sell or buy.

The Influence of Central Banks

Each national government has some mechanism in place to control its supply of currency. Most countries have central or national banks that play a vital role in currency markets. The most influential central banks have the authority to lower and raise interest rates in an effort to control their nation's money supply. By lowering interest rates, a central bank makes it easier to borrow money in that country, stimulating economic growth and consumption. Raising the interest rates slows growth and inflation. In general, the market reacts favorably to lower interest rates and cautiously to rising interest rates. There are situations when rising interest rates attract money into the economy and raise the value of a currency. For example, if the United States pays interest at 1 percent for deposits, Canada pays 2 percent, and Germany pays 3 percent, investors will put their money in the European economy to receive the most favorable return, boosting the value of the euro. The extent to which the euro's value will increase depends on market perception of how long the higher interest rate will last and the number of investors who take advantage of the opportunity. *For more information on global central banks, see Appendix E.*

Other Financial Entities that Influence the Currency Market

Most countries have a government agency responsible for overseeing the trading of securities and protecting investors from fraud. That oversight is primarily directed at the futures and forwards markets, not the spot-cash market used in forex; however, there is movement toward establishing controls over the forex market in the United States and possibly other nations. Some important financial entities that influence the currency market in the United States are:

National Futures Association (NFA)

The National Futures Association (NFA) (**www.nfa.futures.org**) is a self-regulated organization, based in the United States, which provides regulatory programs, market integrity, and oversight to industry-wide futures and forex markets. Although the NFA establishes rules to govern the forex market, these rules are not laws. Participants in the forex market should deal only with companies that have some level of designation from the NFA. The NFA has been relatively successful in convincing companies in the industry to register with the organization and abide by established rules. However, many companies have not become members of the organization. These non-member companies are considered to be unregulated, and their currencies should be avoided.

The NFA also maintains a list of companies that have been disciplined for practicing sales fraud. According to the NFA, a company that has been disciplined is permanently barred from the market for engaging in deceptive telemarketing practices and using deceptive promotional materials. You can find a list of disciplined companies on the NFA website.

Commodity Futures Trading Commission (CFTC)

The Commodity Futures Trading Commission (CFTC) (**www.cftc.gov**) is a government body that monitors the activities of the NFA. The CFTC has jurisdiction over futures and forex markets but does not establish rules for forex trading. That responsibility belongs to the NFA. The CFTC's regulatory authority is limited with respect to retail, over-the-counter forex markets in the United States. Though no single entity has direct regulatory control of the forex market, the CFTC has begun to take on that role. The CFTC is granted authority to regulate the sale of retail, over-the-counter forex futures and options but only for regulated financial entities such as broker-dealers, futures commission merchants (FCMs), banks, and financial institutions. The CFTC also has the authority to abolish unregulated forex entities, particularly unregulated FCMs.

Securities and Exchange Commission (SEC)

The Securities and Exchange Commission (SEC) (**www.sec.gov**) exists to protect investors; maintain fair, efficient, and orderly markets; and to facilitate the formation of capital to sustain economic growth. The SEC oversees securities, securities brokers and dealers, mutual funds, exchanges, and investment advisers. The SEC is concerned with maintaining fair dealing practices, promoting the disclosure of market-related information, and protecting market participants against fraud. In the United States, laws and rules governing the securities industry dictate that all investors should have access to information about investments before buying and for as long as they hold the particular investments. Public firms must regularly disclose meaningful financial information and other important information to the public. The SEC prosecutes hundreds of civil enforcement actions against both companies and individuals each year for crimes such as insider trading, providing false or misleading information, and accounting fraud. The SEC continually reviews feedback from market participants, particularly investors, and investigates questionable market activity. Information about investigations and companies that have been censured can be found on the SEC's website.

Foreign regulatory agencies

Agencies with similar regulatory functions in other nations include:

- Australian Securities and Investment Commission (ASIC) (**www.asic.gov.au/asic/asic.nsf**): An independent government body responsible for regulating financial markets, futures, securities, and corporations.

- Investment Industry Regulatory Organization of Canada (IIROC) (**www.iiroc.ca/English/Pages/home.aspx**): A national self-regulatory member organization for the Canadian securities industry.

- Securities and Futures Commission of Hong Kong (SFC) (**www.sfc.hk/sfc/html/EN**): An independent non-governmental statutory body that has jurisdiction over securities and futures markets in the city of Hong Kong.

- Swiss Federal Banking Commission (SFBC) (**www.finma. ch/archiv/ebk/e/index.html**): An independent administrative authority of the Confederation that supervises particular areas of the Switzerland financial sector.

- Financial Service Authority of the United Kingdom (FSA) (**www.fsa.gov.uk**): A non-government, independent organization that has regulated the financial services industry in the United Kingdom since 2000.

- Bank for International Settlements (BIS) (**www.bis.org**): An international organization that promotes international financial and monetary cooperation. The BIS serves as a bank for the central banks. The BIS is headquartered in Switzerland with two offices in Hong Kong and Mexico City.

The International Monetary Fund

The International Monetary Fund (IMF) (**www.imf.org**) was founded in 1944 to prevent the market fluctuations that occurred before World War II. During this period, each nation had devalued its currency to make its exports more competitive, resulting in shattered economies and social unrest. To avoid further destructive competition, the IMF was given the responsibility of ensuring that member nations implemented a stable exchange rate and balance of payments. If a country suffers economic hardship, the IMF provides that country with a loan to avoid an upset of the global economy. These loans, funded by member nations, are also called tranches and may be granted routinely or on an emergency basis.

The IMF is a controversial institution. Though it is responsible for assisting nations, it is criticized for lending too much money, lending too little money, intervening too late, intervening too early, being too strict, being too lax, and subsidizing risky behavior. The most important aspect of an IMF intervention is that the nation in question is facing serious economic hardship.

The size of a tranche to any given country is determined by the size of the country's economy and its foreign reserves. Quotas are established for each nation. The six largest quotas are established for the United States, Great Britain, Japan, France, Germany, and Saudi Arabia. Each country is allowed to borrow up to 100 percent of its established quota. The first tranche received by a nation is typically provided with lenient terms, and successive tranches require stricter qualifications. Like any other creditor, the more funds the IMF loans to a nation, the more control it requires over its investment. The IMF might impose higher interest rates and a more balanced deficit. Because a nation's economy is in crisis, and the nation is often on the verge of political revolt by the time it seeks assistance from the IMF, these tight controls are unpopular, but the nation often has no other alternative.

Private banks

Private banks play several roles in currency markets, handling large trades for corporations and acting as middlemen for millions of dollars in currency transactions. Most large banks provide traders with money to trade or trade among themselves for speculative profit. These transactions are usually brokered directly over the phone and not open to the public.

Corporations

Larger, multi-national corporations are big players in currency markets. The purchase or sale of manufactured goods or commodities in foreign countries must be translated into domestic currency and included in the company's balance sheet. Because currency fluctuations can wipe out profits if the domestic currency is failing, corporations purchase enough of the foreign currencies to offset potential losses — a process known as hedging. Hedging ensures that if the domestic currency falls, the company will be able to make up for its business losses by selling the foreign currency at a profit. If the domestic currency strengthens, business profits will more than compensate for any losses from currency trades. Corporations may influence currency price fluctuations by adding billions of dollars worth of currencies to the market for either sale or purchase. Corporations also engage directly in currency trading, and some corporations make as much money trading currencies as they do selling their products and services.

Currency traders

Currency traders may be divided into two main groups: hedgers and speculators. Hedgers include companies and governments that buy or sell goods and services in foreign countries and must convert foreign currency into their own domestic currency. Hedgers trade currencies in an effort to protect their sales of goods and services from adverse currency fluctuations in foreign markets. A company located in the United Kingdom, for example, may sell GB pounds and buy U.S. dollars to hedge, or protect, its profits from a fall in the pound. Hedging accounts for about 5 percent of the currency trade volume.

Speculators are banks, home-based operators, and other investors who trade currencies for profit. Speculators simultaneously buy one currency and sell another for profit. Speculation accounts for about 95 percent of the currency trade volume.

Chapter 2

Central Banks

Most central banks will intervene in foreign exchange matters to manipulate interest rates in an attempt to control inflation — one of economic policy makers' greatest fears. Lower interest rates tend to increase the affordability and availability of credit, which has the effect of putting more cash into the money supply. The extra cash available for goods and services increases the demand for them. As demand increases, so do the prices of goods and services, fueling inflation. A central bank's effort to raise interest rates during an inflationary period might have the effect of boosting the economy, or it could further confirm that the nation is already in an inflationary state, causing market fear. When a currency loses value because of inflation, that currency typically takes a loss in the currency market.

Some central banks, such as the U.S. Federal Reserve (Fed), the European Central Bank (ECB), the Bank of Japan (BOJ), the Bank of England (BOE), the Swiss National Bank (SNB), the Bank of Canada (BOC), the Reserve Bank of Australia (RBA), and the Reserve Bank of New Zealand (RBNZ), have a reputation for moving the currency market. Other central banks lack sound leadership and the financial strength necessary to influence the market. A currency's impact on market movements can be understood by analyzing the general economic characteristics of the currencies used by influential central banks.

U.S. Federal Reserve Bank

The U.S. Congress established the Federal Reserve Bank, "the Fed," in 1913. It is independent from the federal government, except that it is subject to oversight by Congress, which periodically reviews its activities. Decisions made by or on behalf of the Fed do not have to be ratified by the President or any other government entity. Congress also divided the United States into 12 districts and established a District Federal Reserve Bank in each of the districts (a map of these districts can be viewed at **www.federalreserve.gov/otherfrb.htm**). Further, the President has the responsibility of appointing a seven-member Board of Governors of the Fed to oversee these district banks. Each member of the Board of Governors is appointed for a 14-year term. The relatively long-term appointment is intended to ensure stability and independence between presidents, who are limited to two four-year terms in office. The president appoints the chairman of the Board for a term of four years, but the appointed term is renewable after the initial four years have expired.

Before the establishment of the Fed, the United States had no formal organization to study and implement monetary policies. The public had little faith in the banking system, and markets were unstable. The Fed acts as a central organization to promote a sound banking system and a healthy economy. It serves as a banker to banks and to the government and is the nation's money manger. It regulates financial institutions; promotes growth, employment, and price stability; moderates long-term interest rates; and issues all paper and coin currency. Though the U.S. Treasury actually produces the nation's currency, the Fed is responsible for the distribution of currency to financial institutions. The Fed also checks currency for wear and tear and removes damaged bills from circulation.

Each of the Fed's district banks generates income from services provided to banks — from foreign currencies held, from interest earned on government securities, and from interest on loans to depository institutions. Income is used to finance the day-to-day operations of the banks, and any excess income is deposited with the U.S. Treasury.

The Fed publishes the biannual *Monetary Policy Report* in February and July. It provides Federal Open Market Committee (FOMC) forecasts for inflation, unemployment, and gross domestic product (GDP) growth. The Fed also participates in the Humphrey-Hawkins testimony, which follows soon after publication. During this testimony, the Fed chairman personally responds to questions posed by Congress and banking committees, with regard to information published in the *Monetary Policy Report*.

The Fed is governed by a mandate that establishes its long-term objective to create price stability and sustain economic growth. This is accomplished through monetary policies that limit inflation and unemployment to achieve balanced growth. The Fed has a reputation for reacting aggressively to economic changes and engaging in open market operations that provide for the purchase of government securities to manipulate interest rates and the federal funds rate, either to reduce inflation or promote growth and consumption.

Federal Open Market Committee (FOMC)

The Fed sets and implements monetary policy through the Federal Open Market Committee (FOMC), which is responsible for establishing short-term interest rates in the United States. Therefore, the Fed is the most watched bank in the world, not just by Congress, but also by a multitude of entities around the globe. The president of the New York Federal Reserve Bank, presidents of four other district banks, and each of the seven members of the Federal Reserve's Board of Governors serve on the FOMC.

The New York Federal Reserve Bank (**www.newyorkfed.org/about-thefed/fedpoint/fed44.html**) is responsible for intervening in foreign exchange markets by buying or selling U.S. dollars to raise or lower the price. The presidents of the four other district banks serve on the FOMC on a one-year rotating basis. The FOMC meets every month to review and discuss the economy and policy. All Fed bank presidents participate in policy-making discussions, and each board member is allowed one vote in establishing economic policy.

Federal Reserve Board (FRB)

The Fed's Federal Reserve Board (FRB) is responsible for supervising and regulating banks. The FRB monitors domestic banks, international banking facilities, foreign activities of foreign member banks, and U.S. activities of foreign banks. The FRB helps to ensure that banks act in the best interest of the public by assisting in the development of federal consumer credit laws, such as the Equal Credit Opportunity Act, the Truth in Savings Act, and the Truth in Lending Act. The FRB also sets margin requirements for investors to limit the amount borrowed for the purchase of securities — stocks, bonds, and other investment instruments. The current requirement is set at 50 percent, which places a limit on a $5,000 investment to $10,000 worth of securities.

U.S. Treasury

While the Fed is responsible for implementing monetary policy, the U.S. Treasury manages fiscal policy, which includes determining the appropriate levels of government spending, and taxation. Therefore, the Treasury actually determines U.S. policy regarding intervention to raise or lower the relative value of the U.S. dollar. The Treasury is also the government entity that assesses economic conditions and gives the Fed the authority and direction to intervene in the foreign exchange market. The overall goal, of both the Fed and the Treasury, is to maintain a strong U.S. dollar.

The U.S. dollar

The most liquid and most frequently traded currency pairs in the foreign exchange market include the U.S. dollar. These currency pairs include:

- USD/JPY
- USD/CHF
- USD/CAN
- EUR/USD
- GBP/USD
- AUD/USD

More than 90 percent of all currency trades involve the U.S. dollar, making it one of the most important currencies in foreign exchange. As a result, U.S. dollar fundamentals cause more market movement than other economic data. *See Chapter 5 for a discussion of currency fundamentals.*

Before the terrorist attack on Sept. 11, 2001, the U.S. dollar was considered a safe haven for currencies, because the risk of dollar instability was perceived as low within the trading community, particularly among global central banks. The United States was considered the safest and most developed market in the world, able to capitalize on its status and attract foreign investments at discounted rates of return. Seventy-six percent of global currency reserves were held in U.S. dollars. Since Sept. 11, 2001, the United States has suffered increasing uncertainty and reduced its interest rates. Foreign investors and foreign central banks, which were invested in U.S. assets, cut back their U.S. holdings. At the same time, the euro gained precedence as a premier reserve currency and as a threat to the stability of the U.S. dollar. Central banks have begun to diversify their reserves and increase their euro holdings while decreasing U.S. dollar holdings, creating one of the most closely watched market trends currently.

The USD relationship to gold

Historically, the U.S. dollar and gold prices have had an inverse relationship, with the value of the dollar increasing when gold prices decreased. Likewise, the dollar value would decrease if gold prices increased. Because gold is measured in dollars, and it is considered a premier safe haven commodity (the ultimate form of money), uncertainty in the United States has led many investors to invest in gold, thereby depreciating the value of the U.S. dollar.

Pegging the U.S. dollar

Many currencies are pegged to the U.S. dollar because of its historic stability and safe-haven status. Pegging means the U.S. government agrees to maintain the dollar as a reserve currency by offering to buy or sell any amount of a foreign nation's domestic currency at an established peg rate. The pegged central bank, in return, agrees to hold U.S. dollars as a reserve currency in amounts at least equal to the amount of domestic currency in circulation. Central banks that are pegged to the U.S. dollar become large holders of U.S. dollars that the central bank is free to manage. The current trend in reserve diversification and toward more flexibility in exchange rates means many central banks may no longer need to peg their currencies with the U.S. dollar in the future.

The U.S. Dollar Index

The U.S. Dollar Index (USDX) is a gauge of the overall strength or weakness of the U.S. dollar. The index is calculated as a trade-weighted average of the currencies of six geometrically different markets. The USDX is also a futures contract traded on the New York Board of Trade. When the news reports a weakness of the dollar or a decline in the trade-weighted dollar, it is usually referring to this index. When the dollar is moving in one direction or another against a particular currency, a trade-weighted average may not show the same movement. Some central banks choose to base their decisions on the USDX, rather than individual performances of currency pairs that include the U.S. dollar.

Currency weighting in the U.S. Dollar Index

Currency	Symbol	Weight in USDX
Euro	EUR	57.6%
Japanese yen	JPY	13.6%
British pound	GBP	11.9%
Canadian dollar	CAD	9.1%
Swedish krona	SEK	4.2%
Swiss franc	CHF	3.6%

The USD relationship to stocks and bonds

U.S. currency, like many other currencies, has a strong correlation with fixed income and equity markets. In general, when U.S. equity markets are rising, foreign investors who seek to profit by investing in U.S. markets need U.S. dollars. When U.S. equity markets fail, domestic investors attempt to sell their shares of local, publicly traded firms and take advantage of foreign investment opportunities, selling U.S. dollars and buying foreign currencies in the process. Fixed-income markets that offer the highest yields are more likely to attract foreign investment dollars. Fluctuations and new development that create movement in these markets require foreign exchange transactions. Any cross-border corporate merger and acquisition (M&A) activities, particularly those that involve cash transactions, will affect the currencies of all markets involved, because the acquiring party will need to buy and sell currency to fund the acquisition.

Differentials, the differences between foreign interest rates and U.S. interest rates, are closely examined when there are yield movements in government bonds and assets. The strength of the U.S. dollar and the yield on return of U.S. assets are related to the interest rate differential between U.S. treasuries and foreign bonds. The differential provides an indication of potential currency movements. Because the U.S. market is one of the largest global markets, investors pay close attention to the yields that are offered for assets. Investors are always seeking the largest possible yields. If U.S. yields increase and/or foreign yields decrease, investors are more inclined to purchase U.S. assets, which increases the strength of the U.S. dollar. On the other hand, if the U.S. yields decrease and/or foreign yields increase, investors might sell their U.S. assets and purchase foreign assets, sparking currency-trading activity.

European Central Bank (ECB)

The European Central Bank (ECB) is the European equivalent of the U.S. Federal Reserve Bank. The ECB determines monetary policy for nations participating in the Economic Monetary Union (EMU). The ECB includes a governing council, which consists of a six-member executive board and 12 governors of national banks. The six members of the executive board include the president and vice president of the ECB, along with four other members. The executive board implements policies dictated by the governing council. The council is the highest decision-making body of the ECB and determines the interest rate banks are charged for borrowing currency from the national banks. The interest rates established by the Council are as closely watched as Fed interest rates.

The six-member executive board is appointed by agreement with the 12 euro nations. The ECB also works with banks that are closely tied to Europe but are not using the euro currency. These nations include Great Britain, Sweden, and Denmark. The combination of the 12 euro nations and the three non-euro nations is known as the Eurosystem. The ECB meets biweekly and has the power to change monetary policy during meetings by a majority vote. The president is given the deciding vote in the case of a tie. Typically, monetary policy changes are only implemented when an official press conference is scheduled to follow the meeting.

The primary goal of the EMU is to maintain price stability and promote growth. Monetary and fiscal policies are implemented to meet this goal. The ECB attempts to maintain an annual growth in its Harmonized Index of Consumer Prices (HICP) below 2 percent and to establish its measure of money supply (M3) to a growth of about 4.5 percent. The ECB uses open market operations and a minimum bid rate, known as the repo rate, to control monetary policy. Open market operations provide refinancing options and management of liquidity. The ECB minimum bid rate provides a target for monetary policy and establishes a level of borrowing for central banks that are members of the ECB.

The Maastricht Treaty

In 1992, the Maastricht Treaty established the European Union and set preconditions for member nations wishing to join the EMU. Each member nation must meet strict requirements to assist the EU in achieving its goal of addressing inflation and deficits. Deviations can result in hefty fines against the offending nation.

The conditions are:

- Member nations must have a general government deficit that does not exceed 3 percent of the GDP, although small, temporary excesses of the deficit will be permitted.

- Member nations must have an overall government debt to GDP ratio of not more than 60 percent. A higher ratio would be considered if such a ratio were shown to be decreasing sufficiently.

- Member nations must have a rate of inflation no more than 1.5 percent above of the average rate of inflation for the three best-performing member nations. The average considers the 12-month rates that precede the assessment.

- In the preceding 12-month period, member nations must have had long-term interest rates not in excess of the average rates of the three nations with the lowest inflation rates by more than 2 percent.

- In the preceding two years, member nations must have had exchange rates that fluctuated within margins of the exchange-rate mechanism.

The ECB is a different entity than the European System of Central Banks (ESCB). Both are independent institutions — independent of national governments and other institutions of the EU. Independence grants these entities the right to control monetary policy according to the terms of the Maastricht Treaty. The treaty states that any member of the decision-making bodies cannot seek or take instruction from any other institution, government of a member state, or any other body.

The euro

The establishment of the euro, which replaced all currencies of nations belonging to the EMU, made the EUR/USD cross currency the most liquid currency in the world. The movement of this cross currency is thought to gauge the economic health of both the United States and Europe. The euro is also known as the anti-dollar because movement of the EUR/USD currency pair has been dictated by dollar fundamentals in recent years. EUR/JPY and EUR/CHF are also very liquid currencies that are used to gauge the general health of the Japanese and Swiss economies. The EUR/USD and EUR/GBP cross currencies provide the greatest trade advantage, as the pairs make orderly moves, have tight spreads, and rarely gap.

As a relatively new currency, the euro is associated with several unique risks that are uncharacteristic of other currencies. Likewise, the ECB's short history makes it difficult for market participants to predict how the bank will react to political and economic changes. The euro is currency for some of the largest European nations and nations of great importance to trading, such as France, Germany, Italy, and Spain. As a result, the euro is vulnerable to any political, social, or economic instability in these individual nations.

The Stability and Growth Pact

The ECB established a Stability and Growth Pact, outlining rules to safeguard sound government finances in member nations. In 2004, these rules were breached by several members, and the ECB has yet to impose any type of restrictions on countries that breached the rules. A newly revised EU constitution, which could provide nations the opportunity to escape penalty if they breach the established budget deficits, has been rejected by some member nations. Legalization of breaches of the Pact has led to a lack of confidence in the euro and the ECB. Some nations, such as Italy, have considered dropping the euro and returning to their original currency.

TIP: Weaker EU economies undermine the credibility of the Stability and Growth Pact.

An article in *Forbes* on January 15, 2010, suggested that Greece's excessive public debt is a threat to the credibility of the euro. By associating themselves with stronger European economies, Greece and other EU members with weaker currencies have benefited from higher credit ratings and lower interest rates for public debt. As a consequence, the Greek government did not feel enough pressure to act responsibly in reigning in the budget deficit. The Maastricht Treaty requires that member nations not have a government deficit that exceeds 3 percent of the nation's GDP. However, Greece has met the criteria only once since it joined the EU in 2001. In 2009, Greece's budget deficit was estimated at 13.6 percent of its GDP. Private investors are becoming nervous about buying the bonds the Greek government must sell to maintain its public debt. Because the ECB is not allowed to bail out its members in a crisis, one of the EU member nations or the IMF would have to offer Greece an emergency loan. A situation like that would greatly diminish confidence in the euro and in the ability of the EU to enforce its economic standards. Strict enforcement might hamper the economic growth that Greece needs to reduce its public debt, but lack of enforcement will weaken the euro.

The Euro's relationship to stocks and bonds

The ten-year German bund is considered the benchmark bond for the European community. Ten-year U.S. government bonds may be used to predict the future of euro exchange rates, particularly exchange rates against the U.S. dollar. The differential between ten-year German bunds and ten-year U.S. government bonds is thought to provide the best indicator of euro movement. When bund rates exceed Treasury rates and the differential increases or spreads widen, the euro is looked on as a bullish market. If the differential decreases or the spread tightens, the market is perceived as a bear market.

The Euribor rate

The euro interbank offer rate, also known as the Euribor rate, is a three-month fixed interest rate offered from one large eurozone bank to another on interbank term deposits. Currency traders compare the Euribor futures rate with the Eurodollar futures rate. Eurodollars are U.S. dollars deposited at foreign banks and other foreign financial institutions. When the spread between Eurodollars and Euribor futures widens in favor of the Euribor, investors tend to invest in European fixed assets, creating a demand for euros. In recent years, merger and acquisition (M&A) activities have increased between the EU and the United States. M&A activities that involve large amounts of cash may have a significant short-term impact on EUR/USD movements.

Bank of Japan (BOJ)

Japan is the world's third-largest economy. The Bank of Japan (BOJ), the primary fiscal policy-making body for the nation of Japan, has operational independence from Japan's Ministry of Finance (MOF) and, consequently, has complete control of monetary policy. However, the MOF has control of foreign exchange policy and directs the BOJ in executing all foreign exchange transactions. A nine-member board, known as the Policy Board, directs the BOJ. It includes the BOJ governor, two deputy governors, and six others who are selected based on their experiences or expertise in Japan's economics. However, the Japanese government often intervenes to keep the yen at favorable rates and to ensure that Japanese exports remain competitive.

Over the past decade, Japan has experienced an economic crisis. In an attempt to develop new initiatives to stimulate growth, the BOJ holds monetary policy meetings twice a month, immediately followed by press releases and briefings. The BOJ also publishes a *Monthly Report of Recent Economic and Financial Developments,* announcing new monetary or fiscal policies and any changes in sentiment of the BOJ. Because the MOF directs foreign exchange matters, comments from officials of the MOF are also closely watched.

Exports are the biggest contributor to the Japanese economy, so the government favors a weakened yen. If the Japanese yen experiences a significant or fast-paced appreciation, the MOF and BOJ voice their concerns, but if there is no action by government, the market becomes immune to warnings. The history of intervention in Japan's currency markets has resulted in active manipulation of the Japanese yen through open-market operations.

The Japanese yen

Japan, with the largest per capita GDP in Asia, is used to gauge the broader strength of the Asian economy. Japan has the most developed capital markets, which have historically attracted investors to Asia. Japan conducts significant trade with other Asian nations; therefore, the economic and political problems that plague Japan negatively affect other countries. Likewise, political and economic problems of these other nations have an impact on Japan and movement of the yen.

The MOF and BOJ are important institutions that have the ability to move markets. The MOF is the director of foreign exchange interventions, and as a result, comments from MOF officials provide significant information. The BOJ and MOF have a long history of entering foreign exchange markets when they are dissatisfied with the level of the Japanese yen. Japan's economy is closely tied to political officials and heads of large corporations who are interested in keeping the yen at low levels to lower the prices of their exports. The MOF is in tune with political officials and corporate heads when it decides to intervene to depreciate a strong yen. The BOJ periodically receives information on large hedge fund positions from banks and will intervene when speculators are on the other side of the market.

There are three main factors behind MOF and BOJ interventions. First, intervention is sought when the yen moves by seven or more yen within a period of less than six weeks. Using USD/JPY as a reference, seven yen is equivalent to 700 pips. Secondly, interventions to depreciate a strong yen occur above USD/JPY 115 level in only 11 percent of all BOJ interventions. Thirdly, the BOJ and MOF intervene when market participants are holding positions in the opposite direction to maximize the impact of intervention.

Toward the end of the Japanese fiscal year on March 31, Japanese cross currency pairs become very active. During this time, exporters convert their dollar-denominated assets to Japanese yen. Doing so helps Japanese banks rebuild their balance sheets to meet guidelines of the Financial Services Authority (FSA) that require that banks mark security holdings to market. In anticipation of the exporters' need to repatriate dollar assets, speculators may bid the yen higher in value in an attempt to take advantage of the increased inflow of currency. Following the end of the fiscal year, speculators close their positions, and the Japanese yen tends to bias toward depreciation.

In addition to the active year-end crosses, time plays a role in day-to-day trading activities. Japanese traders usually take one-hour lunches between 10 p.m. and 11 p.m. EST, leaving junior and less experienced traders to handle their affairs. As a result, the Japanese yen may become volatile, or fluctuate frequently, during this time, because the market tends to become very liquid. With the exception of lunch hour, the Japanese market moves in a relatively orderly fashion, unless some government statement, breaking news, or surprising economic data is released.

However, there is some increased volatility during U.S. trading hours, because U.S. traders actively trade both U.S. and Japanese positions.

Bank of England (BOE)

The Bank of England (BOE) was established in 1694 and is the second-oldest central bank in the world. The bank was initially established to provide government loans but later expanded to provide credit to the nation's banking system. In 1946, the bank was nationalized and operated strictly under government control. In 1997, the bank became free of this governmental control. As an independent entity, the BOE established the Monetary Policy Board, which operates similarly to the Fed's FOMC. The Monetary Policy Committee (MPC) consists of nine members who set monetary policy for the United Kingdom. The BOE is responsible for setting interest rates, managing the United Kingdom's foreign exchange and gold reserves, and managing the government's stock register.

The MPC is granted operational independence in establishing monetary policy for the United Kingdom. The committee consists of a governor, two deputy governors, two executive directors of the central bank, and four outside experts. Monetary policy is usually centered on achieving an inflation target, as set by the treasury chancellor. The target is determined by the value of the United Kingdom's retail price index — exclusive (RPI-X), which is the RPI exclusive of mortgage payments. The current target is 2.5 percent growth in RPI-X. The BOE may change interest rates to meet this target rate. The MPC holds monthly meetings, and market participants watch for announcements on monetary policy. They publish statements after every meeting, plus a quarterly inflation report that details the MPC's predictions for growth and inflation over the next two years as well as justification for any policy changes. The MPC also publishes a *Quarterly Bulletin* that documents past monetary policy movements and provides an analysis of the international economic environment and its impact on the U.K. economy.

The British pound

U.K. currency has three names that are used interchangeably — the British pound, sterling, and the cable. The British pound is one of the four most liquid currencies available to trade. About 18 percent of all currency trades involve the British pound as either the base or quote currency. The United Kingdom's highly developed capital markets are partly responsible for the high liquidity. GBP/USD is more liquid than EUR/GBP, but EUR/GBP is the leading measure of U.K. economic strength because GBP/USD tends to be more sensitive to U.S. developments. EUR/GBP is a more fundamental trade, because Europe is the United Kingdom's primary trade and investment partner. The United Kingdom and Europe's currencies are interdependent, with movements in the EUR/GBP possibly affecting movements in the GBP/USD, and vice versa. Traders who trade U.K. pounds need to stay abreast of both currency pairs. The rate of EUR/GBP should always be exactly equal to EUR/USD divided by GBP/USD. Even the smallest deviations from this ratio are exploited by market participants and quickly eliminated.

The GBP relationship to oil

Some of the largest energy companies in the world are located in the United Kingdom. Energy production represents 4 percent of the United Kingdom's GDP. As a result, the British pound is positively correlated with energy pricing. Many member nations of the EU import oil from the United Kingdom and as oil prices increase these nations have to purchase more U.K. pounds to pay for purchases. The United Kingdom's oil exporters then benefit from the increased earnings as the value of the U.K. pound increases relative to other currencies.

Speculation for U.K. differentials

Many investors who seek investment opportunities outside of the United States choose to invest in the United Kingdom's highly developed markets. The pound has experienced some of the highest interest rates among developed nations. Although Australia and New Zealand have offered higher rates of interest, these nations do not have well-developed markets. Many investors who have existing positions or are interested in initiating new positions use the British pound to place long positions against U.S., Japanese, and Swiss currencies.

The increase in carry trades has also increased demand for the British pound. Carry trades involve borrowing and selling a low-interest currency and using the capital to buy a higher yielding currency, or lending a currency with a higher yield and selling a lower yielding currency. Traders take positions in carry trades to profit from the interest rate differential. However, a significant number of carry traders could increase the volatility of the British pound if the yield differential between the British pound and other currencies narrow.

The GBP relationship to stocks and bonds

Market participants use interest differentials between U.K. fixed interest rate bonds (gilts) and other foreign bonds to gauge monetary flows. Interest rate differentials between U.K. gilts and U.S. treasuries may be used to gauge GBP/USD flows. Interest rate differentials between U.K. gilts and German bunds may be used to gauge EUR/GBP flows. The German bund is often used as the basis for European yields. Investors use these differentials as indicators of the potential of capital flows or currency movements. Interest rate differentials also may be used to gauge the premium yield that U.K. fixed income assets are offering instead of U.S. and European fixed income assets, or vice versa. The United Kingdom has a reputation for providing competitive yields while also providing safety of stability standard equivalent to the United States.

U.K. bank repo rate

The bank repo rate is the interest rate used in monetary policy. Though in most nations market participants gain insight into any bias toward rate changes by assessing comments from government officials, the BOE requires members of the Monetary Policy Committee to publish their voting records. Their individual accountability in monetary policy is used to assure market participants that comments represent the opinions of individual committee members, not the opinions of the BOE. Market participants must look elsewhere to find indications of potential rate movements of the BOE. Three-month futures contracts of the euro vs. U.K. pound sterling reflect market expectations of the euro vs. U.K. pound sterling interest rate three months into the future. These contracts also anticipate U.K. interest rate changes that affect fluctuations of the GBP/USD.

The U.K. currency market is affected by any comments, speeches, or polls, particularly those made by the prime minister or treasury chancellor. Any indication that the U.K. might decide to adopt the euro as its currency usually leads to downward pressure on the GBP, while opposition to the adoption tends to boost the GBP because interest rates would have to decrease significantly to bring the GBP into line with the euro. An interest rate decrease would cause carry trade investors to close their positions or sell their British pounds. GBP/USD would decline because of uncertainty in euro adoptions. The United Kingdom and the British pound have performed well under the existing monetary authority. With 12 nations under one monetary authority, the EMU has not yet proven it is capable of implementing a monetary policy suitable for its existing member nations. The EMU is experiencing many difficulties with its existing member nations breaching established criteria.

Swiss National Bank (SNB)

The Swiss National Bank (SNB) is an independent central bank with a three-member board, known as the Governing Board of the SNB. The board has a chairman, vice chairman, and one other member who are responsible for determining monetary policy. All decisions are subject to a consensus vote — the option with the most votes is the consensus. The board meets once per quarter to review monetary policy, but decisions on monetary policy may be announced at any time. Unlike some other central banks, the SNB does not set a single interest rate target. Instead, a target range is established by the three-month Swiss LIBOR rate. Monetary targets are also important as indicators because they may provide insight on long-term inflation, but the SNB focuses on the inflation target, which is set at less than 2 percent per year, a measure based on the national consumer index. To speed up the Swiss economy, the SNB lowers the interest rate. When it looks like the economy is expanding and inflation will exceed 2.5 percent, the SNB loosens its monetary policies and allows interest rates to rise. The SNB monitors exchange rates as well as rates of inflation because strength in the Swiss franc could lead to inflation. In particular, when global risk aversion causes capital flows into Switzerland to increase, the SNB, which generally favors a weak franc, will intervene to provide liquidity in the franc, through SNB officials' commenting on the currency, liquidity, and the money supply.

The Swiss franc

The unique characteristic of the Swiss franc is its safe-haven status. The Swiss history of political neutrality, and the banking system's policy of protecting the identity of its investors, make Switzerland the world's largest destination for offshore capital. The Swiss franc tends to move based on foreign economic and political events, rather than domestic conditions. In times of global instability and uncertainty, investors invest in Switzerland. The goal of these investors is retention of their investment dollars, rather than appreciation of the investment amount. Funds will flow into Switzerland to take advantage of the safe-haven status, causing the Swiss franc to appreciate, or gain in value, regardless of whether monetary growth is achievable.

Members of the EU have persistently pressured Switzerland to relax its practice of protecting confidentiality in its banking system and allow increased transparency of its customer accounts. The EU attributes tax evasion and difficulties prosecuting tax evaders to the confidentiality of the Swiss banking system and, therefore, has threatened to impose sanctions on Switzerland. Switzerland has refused to comply with such requests because confidentiality is the core strength of its banking system. Political entities in both the EU and Switzerland are negotiating for an equitable resolution.

The CHF relationship to gold

Switzerland is the seventh-largest holder of gold in the world. Traditionally, the Swiss constitution mandated that at least 40 percent of its currency be backed by gold reserves, but a constitutional amendment in 1997 changed it to 25 percent. Although the Swiss constitution changed this mandate, the positive correlation between gold and the Swiss franc remains in the neighborhood of 80 percent. If gold appreciates, the Swiss franc is most likely to appreciate in response. Because gold is considered the ultimate safe-haven form of money, both the Swiss franc and gold benefit from any global or geographical uncertainty.

Carry trading the Swiss franc

Though Switzerland offers some of the lowest interest rates in the industrialized world, the Swiss franc is a popular choice for carry trades. Carry trades involve buying a currency with a higher interest rate and selling a currency with a lower interest rate to fund the purchase; or lending a currency with a higher interest rate and borrowing a currency with a lower interest rate. Traders sell Swiss francs against a higher yielding currency, usually accomplished with cross currency pairs such as GBP/CHF or AUD/CHF. These trades affect the EUR/CHF and USD/CHF currency pairs. To exit their carry trade positions, traders re-purchase Swiss francs.

The interest rate differential between three-month euro-Swiss futures and Eurodollar futures provides a gauge of Swiss and U.S. money flows. The differential indicates how many more premium-yield, fixed-income assets the Swiss are offering over U.S. fixed income assets, or vice versa. The differential is of particular interest to carry traders who enter and exit the market based on positive interest-rate differentials between international fixed-income assets.

The Swiss franc in M&A activities

Switzerland's primary industry is banking and finance, in which merger and acquisition (M&A) activities are very common. M&A activities, particularly as they involve foreign entities, affect the Swiss franc. A foreign company, for example, must buy Swiss francs and sell its own domestic currency to purchase a Swiss bank. Conversely, if a Swiss bank purchases a foreign company, the Swiss bank must sell Swiss francs and buy the domestic currency of the company's home nation. In either case, M&A activities that involve Swiss banks and companies will significantly affect the movement of the Swiss franc.

The Swiss franc's cross currency relationship

The EUR/CHF is the most commonly traded currency for traders who want to participate in Swiss markets. The USD/CHF is the least frequently traded currency pair for those who want to participate in Swiss markets because it offers higher liquidity and volatility. Day traders may favor the USD/CHF pair over EUR/CHF because of that volatility. During times of global severe risk aversion, the USD/CHF develops a market of its own. The USD/CHF pair is really derived from EUR/USD and EUR/CHF because USD/CHF should be exactly equal to EUR/CHF divided by EUR/USD. Market participants use EUR/USD and EUR/CHF currency pairs to price current levels of USD/CHF when the currency pair is illiquid, and they consider the two currency pairs to be indicators for trading USD/CHF.

Bank of Canada (BOC)

The Bank of Canada (BOC) is focused on maintaining integrity and value of its currency. The board of the BOC, known as the Governing Council of the Bank of Canada, consists of a governor and six deputy governors and is responsible for setting monetary policy. The BOC meets about eight times per year to discuss monetary policy changes and releases a quarterly statement of monthly monetary policy updates.

The BOC ensures price stability by adhering to an inflation target agreed on with the Canadian Department of Finance. The inflation target is 1 percent to 3 percent. The perception of the BOC is that high inflation can be damaging to the nation's economy and low inflation equates with price stability, which is associated with sustainable long-term growth of the economy. The BOC uses short-term interest rates to control inflation. If inflation exceeds the target, the bank implements tighter monetary controls. If inflation is below the target, the bank loosens monetary policy. The BOC has done well with keeping inflation within target.

The BOC changes monetary policies by manipulating the bank interest rate, which affects the exchange rate. These interest rate changes are not really designed to manipulate exchange rates but to control inflation.

The BOC uses the bank rate and open market operations to implement its monetary policy. If currency appreciation reaches undesirable levels, the BOC increases interest rates to offset the rise. If currency depreciation reaches undesirable levels, the BOC raises rates.

Monetary Conditions Index

Monetary conditions are measured by the BOC using its Monetary Conditions Index (MCI). The index is a weighted sum of change in the 90-day commercial paper interest rate and G10 trade-weighted exchange rate. The weight is three-to-one for the commercial paper interest rate versus the G10 trade-weighted exchange rate. The particular weight is chosen because it represents data from historical studies of the effect of changes in interest rates on the exchange rate. In short, a 2 percent increase in short-term interest rates is equivalent to 6 percent appreciation in the trade-weighted exchange rate.

The Canadian dollar

Canada's economy is highly dependent on commodities. Canada is the world's seventh-largest producer of gold and seventh-largest producer of oil. The positive correlation between the Canadian dollar and commodity prices is near 60 percent. Increased commodity prices usually benefit Canada's domestic producers, while also increasing the nation's income from imports. However, strong Canadian commodity prices also have the effect of lessening outside demand for commodities in foreign nations, such as the United States.

The CAD's relationship with the United States

The United States imports 85 percent of Canadian exports. Canada has maintained a merchandise trade surplus with the United States since the 1980s. The account surplus has reached as high as $78 billion. Strong demand from the United States and strong energy prices have led to record-high energy exports, making the Canadian economy sensitive to changes in the U.S. economy. As the U.S. economy grows, trades with Canada increase to benefit the overall Canadian economy. However, a slowdown of the U.S. economy creates a reduction of import activities, which significantly hurts the Canadian economy.

Canada's proximity to the United States makes cross border merger and acquisition (M&A) activity very commonplace. As companies strive to globalize, these types of mergers lead to money flow between foreign nations that affect the currencies of both nations. For example, the significant acquisition of Canadian energy companies has led to the United States' injecting millions of dollars into the Canadian economy, creating a strong growth in USD/CAD because U.S. companies have to sell U.S. dollars and purchase Canadian dollars to pay for such acquisitions.

Carry trading the CAD

Interest rate differentials between Canadian cash rates and short-term interest rate yields in other nations provide an indication of potential money flows. The differentials indicate how much premium yield the Canadian dollar is offering for short-term fixed assets versus the premium yield for short-term fixed assets of other nations. This is of particular importance to carry traders who enter the market based on positive interest rate differentials between fixed income assets.

The Canadian dollar is a popular currency to use for carry trades with the United States. When Canada offers higher interest rates than the United States, the short USD/CAD carry trade increases in popularity because of the proximity of the two nations. However, if the United States increases rates or Canada reduces its rate, the positive interest rate differential between the Canadian dollar and other currencies narrows and speculators react by exiting their carry trades, which depreciates the Canadian dollar.

Reserve Bank of Australia (RBA)

The Reserve Bank of Australia (RBA) is mandated, through monetary and banking policies, to ensure the stability of the Australian dollar, maintain full employment, and achieve economic prosperity and welfare for the people. The RBA's monetary policy committee consists of a governor or chairman, a deputy governor or vice chairman, a secretary of the treasury, and six independent members who are appointed by the government of Australia. Changes in monetary policy are voted on based on the consensus of the committee. The RBA holds monthly meetings on the first Tuesday of the month, except for January, to discuss potential changes in monetary policy. Following these meetings, the RBA issues a press release that outlines justification for any monetary policy changes. If no change is made, no press release is published. The RBA also publishes the *Reserve Bulletin* monthly. Semi-annual issues of this publication in May and November include a statement on the Conduct of Monetary Policy. Quarterly issues, published in February, May, August, and November, include the Quarterly Report on the economy and financial markets. These publications provide market participants with insight on any potential monetary policy changes.

The government of Australia believes that controlling inflation is the key to long-term sustainable growth. As a result, the government has established an informal consumer price inflation target of 2 percent to 3 percent per year. The inflation target is expected to preserve the value of money, provide discipline in monetary policy decision-making, and provide guidelines for the private sector, relative to inflation expectations. The inflation target also increases the transparency of RBA activities. Market participants know that when inflation or expectations for inflation exceed the target level, the RBA is prepared to intervene to tighten monetary policy with rate hikes.

All Australian interest rates are influenced by the interest rates established for overnight loans in the money market. Monetary policy involves setting interest rates on these overnight loans. Changes in monetary policy affect the interest rate structure of Australian financial systems and also affect the sentiment of currencies, meaning that the behavior of borrowers and lenders in financial markets is affected by this monetary policy. The RBA establishes a cash rate, which is the target rate for open market operations. The cash rate is charged on overnight loans between financial entities, giving the cash rate a close relationship with money market interest rates. There is a strong correlation between interest rate differentials and currency movement.

The Australian dollar

The Australian dollar has a strong correlation with commodity prices, particularly gold prices. Correlations have been measured at about 80 percent. Australia is the world's second-largest gold producer, and gold accounts for about $5.5 billion in exports each year. As a result, the Australian dollar benefits from commodity-price increases. Likewise, it depreciates when commodity prices decrease. When commodity prices are high and the fear of inflation sets in, the RBA may consider increasing interest rates to curb inflation. However, gold prices tend to increase during times of global economic or political uncertainty. The RBA leaves Australia vulnerable to economic decline if it decides to raise interest rates under such conditions, because inflation is not necessarily the source of the problem.

Carry trading the AUD

Australia offers some of the highest interest rates of developing countries and is a popular currency for carry trades because it offers fair, liquid currency. The popularity of carry trades was estimated to have assisted in raising the Australian dollar by about 57 percent against the

U.S. dollar in 2001. Carry trades offer investors high yields when equity investments are offering minimal returns. Carry trades, however, only last as long as the actual yield advantage exists. Should other central banks increase interest rates, and the positive rate differentials between Australia and other nations narrow, the AUD/USD could suffer from an overabundance of carry traders pulling their investments out of Australia in search of higher returns in the United States.

Interest rate differentials between Australian cash rates and short-term foreign interest rate yields are an indicator of potential money flows. The differentials indicate how much premium yield the Australian dollar is offering for short-term fixed assets versus the premium yield for short-term fixed assets of other nations. The yield is of particular importance to carry traders who enter the market based on positive interest rate differentials between fixed-income assets.

Weather conditions affect the AUD

Because commodities account for the majority of Australian exports, the GDP is sensitive to weather conditions such as drought, which may damage farming activities. Agriculture accounts for about 2.5 percent of the GDP. The RBA estimates that a decline in farming activities could directly reduce growth in the GDP by 1 percent. Drought has a direct impact on other aspects of the economy because companies that furnish supplies and services to agricultural producers and retailers in rural farming communities are also affected. Australian history has shown the economy is able to recover strongly after a drought.

Reserve Bank of New Zealand

New Zealand, with a population of only about 4.3 million, maintains tight controls over its economy. The Reserve Bank of New Zealand (RBNZ) is the central bank of New Zealand and has a Monetary Policy

Committee of bank executives who are responsible for reviewing monetary policy on a weekly basis. Meetings of the Monetary Policy Committee are held about every six weeks to decide on changes to monetary policy. The final decision for any rate changes lies with the RBNZ bank governor. Each time a new governor is appointed, he or she establishes a Policy Target Agreement (PTA) with the Finance Minister in an attempt to maintain a stable monetary policy and avoid instability in interest rates, exchange rates, and output. Price stability is achieved by maintaining the yearly Consumer Price Index (CPI) inflation at 1.5 percent. If the RBNZ fails to meet this target, the government has the authority to dismiss the bank governor, although this rarely happens. The authority to do so serves as an incentive to meet the inflation target.

The RBNZ uses an official cash rate (OCR) and open market operations to implement monetary policy changes. The RBNZ pays interest and receives deposits at 25 basis points (a basis point is one hundredth of one percent) below the OCR. They also lend overnight cash at 25 basis points above the OCR rate. The RBNZ can raise or lower the interest rates offered to individuals and companies by controlling the cost of liquidity for commercial banks. The objective is to compete with and attract the customers of banks by offering rates above and below the bounds of the overnight rate. It is anticipated that customers will choose the RBNZ because funds may be borrowed at a lower cost and the yields are higher. The OCR is reviewed and manipulated as appropriate to maintain the economic stability of the nation.

New Zealand open market operations are used to meet the cash target, which is the target amount of reserves held by registered banks. The current target is $20 million New Zealand dollars. The RBNZ forecasts daily fluctuation in the cash target and uses the forecast amount to determine the amount necessary to inject into or withdraw from reserves to meet the target.

New Zealand Treasury

The New Zealand Treasury provides the following objectives as guidelines for fiscal policy measures:

- Expenses should average about 35 percent of the GDP over the time period used to calculate contributions toward future costs of New Zealand Superannuation (NZS), the fund that provides retirement benefits for eligible New Zealanders older than 65. During the buildup of assets to meet future NZS costs, expenses plus contributions should be around 35 percent of the GDP. Over longer terms, expenses minus any withdrawals to meet NZS costs should be about 35 percent of the GDP.

- Revenues should be sufficient to meet the operating balance objective, which is to offer a robust, broad-based tax system that raises revenue in a fair and efficient method.

- An operating surplus should be maintained that, on average over the chosen economic cycle, is sufficient to meet the requirements for contributions toward future NZS costs and is consistent with debt objectives.

- A gross debt below 30 percent of the GDP on average should be maintained over the chosen economic cycle. Net debt excludes assets to meet future NZS costs. Net debt should be less than 20 percent of the GDP on average over the chosen economic cycle.

- Net worth should be consistent with the operating balance objective through a build up of assets to meet future NZS costs.

The New Zealand dollar

New Zealand is a trade-oriented nation, and Australia is New Zealand's biggest trading partner. New Zealand benefits when a strong Australian economy allows Australian companies to increase their import activities. For example, the boom in the Australian housing industry, which began in the late 1990s, required increased imports of building supplies from New Zealand, which fared well from the increased export operations. Australian imports increased by 10 percent between 1999 and 2002. The two nations' currency pairs, NZD/USD and AUD/USD, are almost perfect images of each other, with correlations of the two currency pairs reaching as much as 97 percent.

The NZD relationship to commodities

Commodities represent more than 40 percent of New Zealand's exports, with a 50 percent correlation between the New Zealand dollar and commodity prices. As commodity prices increase, the New Zealand dollar appreciates. However, the correlation between commodity prices and the New Zealand dollar is not totally dependent on New Zealand's trade activities. The performance of the Australian economy is also highly correlated to commodity pricing. As a result, the correlation between the New Zealand dollar and the Australian dollar creates a commodity-linked currency. As commodity prices increase, the Australian economy benefits, translating into increased trade activity, particularly with New Zealand.

Carry trading the NZD

New Zealand offers some of the highest interest rates among industrialized countries, making it a prime candidate for carry trades. The popularity of carry trades has led to a rise in the New Zealand dollar, also making it sensitive to interest rate changes. Should the United States increase interest rates, for example, New Zealand would have to offer competitive interest rates to prevent speculators from reversing their carry trade positions.

Interest rate differentials between the cash rate of the New Zealand dollar and the short-term interest rate yields of other industrialized nations provide good indicators of the potential for money flows. The differentials indicate how much premium yield NZD short-term fixed-income assets offer versus foreign short-term fixed-income assets. Carry traders enter and exit the market based on the positive interest rate differential between global fixed-income assets.

Weather conditions affect the NZD

Like Australia, New Zealand's economy is vulnerable to drought and other bad weather conditions because its economy is driven by exports of commodities. Drought is very common in Australia, New Zealand's largest trading partner, and droughts have historically restricted New Zealand's farming activities. For example, in 1998, New Zealand lost more than NZ$168 million because of drought. Droughts have cost Australia up to a 1 percent loss of its GDP, creating a negative impact on the New Zealand trading activities and economy.

Immigration affects the NZD

New Zealand has a relatively small population, and any increase in immigration has a significant impact on the economy. Even small increases in immigration affect the performance of the economy because a growing population means a greater demand for goods and services.

Even if your forex trading strategy is based entirely on charts and technical patterns, it is important to understand the economic forces that affect the currency pairs you have selected. Historical patterns can change significantly if the economic factors that drive them are altered.

The next chapter describes the forex market and how you, as an individual investor, can participate in it.

Chapter 3

The Forex Market

Traditionally, the only way investors could access the foreign exchange market was through banks that engaged in commercial or investment transactions that included large amounts of currency. In 1971, exchange rates were allowed to float freely, creating opportunities for currency speculators to make a profit by buying a currency and then selling it when its value rose against another currency. The rapid development of the Internet in the 1990s gave rise to forex dealers who broke currency trades down into smaller units and offered them to individual investors. Growth in the forex market resulted directly from the development of online trading platforms and the market's 24-hour availability. Today, anyone with fast Internet access and knowledge of the currency market can trade currencies.

An increase in global trade and foreign investment, coupled with the constant fluctuation of the dollar against other global currencies, has expanded the forex market over the past few decades. Investors are able to realize profits from the forex market when other markets have become unstable because currencies are always rising and falling in value relative to other currencies. The forex market offers advantages in trading that contribute to its potential to generate profits even when the economy is weak. Currency traders may enter and exit the market at will, regardless of market conditions. The liquidity in the market is partly responsible for the large volume of forex trading, in excess of $3 trillion dollars a day. Forex is the most liquid market in the world.

The forex market is composed of a global network of currency dealers, primarily commercial banks that trade and communicate electronically or by telephone. The forex market is an over-the-counter (OTC) market, in which buyers and sellers communicate directly without a centralized system or physical exchange to facilitating transactions. It resembles the bond market or the National Association of Securities Dealers Automatic Quotation System (NASDAQ) market rather than the New York Stock Exchange (NYSE).

Most forex traders do spot trading — the immediate purchase or sale of a currency at a quoted price. Investors interact directly with persons in the market who are responsible for currency pairing. Though most countries have some regulatory control over forex transactions, governmental influence over the forex market is relatively limited compared to the control exercised over other investment markets. As the market continues to expand, it is expected that more governmental controls will be implemented. Currently, the forex market does not require investors to pay government fees, exchange fees, clearing fees, or brokerage fees. In contrast to typical futures markets where the lot and contract sizes are determined by a centralized exchange, spot trading allows investors to trade for lot sizes that require investments of less than $1,000.

The foreign currency market has little correlation with the stock market. The outlook for profit potential is determined by the relative value of one currency against another. When foreign investors see opportunity to profit from rising stock prices in a particular country, they must purchase that country's currency in order to invest. When a country's stock market starts to fall, investors sell their investments and seek new opportunities in other countries. In either a bull market or bear market, opportunities exist for market trading. In a bull market, which has a positive outlook, a currency trader profits by buying currency in the positive market against other currencies. If the economic outlook is not good, a bull market is created for other currencies, and the currency trader profits by selling currency in the pessimistic market against other currencies.

Big central banks, which have historically manipulated prices in other markets, have been unsuccessful in manipulating market prices in forex. The number of participants in the forex market is so large that no single investor can control market price for an extended time. Insider trading and other forms of fraud occur less often than in any other financial market, because the size and nature of the forex market make it difficult for insiders to manipulate pricing information.

The forex market provides for low transaction costs that may be considerably less than those in retail transactions. Under normal market conditions, the retail transaction cost, also known as the bid or ask spread, is typically less than 0.1 percent. Transaction costs for larger currency dealers may be as low as 0.07 percent. Both profit potential and loss potential are amplified by the low margins and high leverage offered in the forex market.

Foreign Exchange Systems

Governments generally follow one of three foreign exchange systems — free float, peg, and dirty float. A free float system lacks any form of government intervention or steering. The market is allowed to adjust prices according to supply and demand. This system provides officials with flexibility in establishing domestic policies and provides the smallest target for speculators. The peg system is also called currency board. Under this system, domestic currency rates are fixed to a single foreign currency or group of currencies. The peg system assists smaller nations and developing economies in providing stability and controlling inflation; it limits flexibility of governments in establishing domestic economic policy and provides speculators with an easy target. The dirty float system incorporates both the free flow and peg systems. It differs from the free float system because prices are not completely driven by market forces. Central banks may intervene in foreign exchange matters to influence currency prices. The dirty float system differs from the peg system because currency is not officially pegged to any particular foreign exchange rate. The dirty float system is the most widely used system because it allows governments to intervene in foreign exchange matters in the best interest of a nation's economy. Intervention occurs when either an official regulatory agency or financial institution directly coerces the currency exchange rate by devaluating or revaluating a currency or by manipulating imports and exports. Intervention affects the market by causing erratic changes in exchange rates and market volatility.

> **TIP: You can profit when a government intervention disrupts the market.**
>
> The erratic market resulting from a government intervention presents an opportunity to profit from price fluctuations if you protect yourself with stop-loss orders.

Though the dirty float system is the most widely used, a peg system can be beneficial to smaller and developing nations. The peg system allows these nations to develop more credible monetary policies by adjusting currency to a more stable and larger currency, thereby controlling inflation, reducing financial costs, having flexibility in lowering interest rates, and spurring economic growth.

A viable peg system must have three primary components:

- An exchange rate anchored to either a single or multiple currencies

- A long-term commitment to the monetary policy of the anchoring nation

- Convertibility to the anchoring currency system

These components give the market assurance that a domestic currency is backed by the anchoring currency of foreign reserves.

A disadvantage of peg systems is that they make easy targets for speculators in foreign exchange. The peg system may also prove to be unstable in the long run. Nations that attempt to strengthen their economies and monetary systems with the use of pegs limit the usefulness of their own monetary and fiscal policy and become dangerously reliant on the anchoring foreign exchange policy.

Interbank versus Retail Forex

The forex market has two tiers: the interbank wholesale market and the retail market. The interbank market accounts for approximately two-thirds of the foreign currency trading volume. It consists of an informal network of brokers and dealers who trade with banks, central banks, and other large financial institutions. More than 200 banks are involved in the interbank market. The trades are based on credit ratings and trading size and are in the hundreds of millions of dollars. Banks typically do not offer price quotes for less than one million units of currency. Most forex traders do not meet the credit and size requirements for trading in the interbank; instead individual traders trade in the retail forex market, also known as the client forex market. About 18 percent of forex trading volume consist of speculators who trade in the retail forex market through an intermediary that moves trades into the interbank market.

There is no physical, centralized location where trade information for the forex market is collected and distributed. Forex traders must study the interbank market to detect supply and demand trends in the market. Information about some currency trades is not available to retail traders until after the trade has been executed. Large trades executed among large banks and financial institutions are quietly voice-brokered over the telephone or through other voice or electronic chat communication.

By the time the public learns about such trades, the participating banks have already anticipated them and adjusted their investments accordingly. Forex is an unregulated market where any two self-regulated agencies may engage in a trade without reporting the details of the trade to a centralized exchange or any other institution. Only the participants know the specifics of the trade, therefore they are the only parties capable of engaging in a trade based on any newly established prices. Banks might be able to detect such trades through the documented banking activity associated with the trade and respond accordingly. For trade information retail investors depend on news feeds, which typically report these types of large trades only after the trade is completed and confirmed. Banking activity like this, though it does not dominate the forex market, plays a critical role in price movement and handicaps the retail trader.

Some of the larger players in currency trading still handle their trades by telephone in an effort to keep their activities private and secure. Even so, modern day trading includes the Internet and evolving technologies that provide retail investors with fast access to the forex market. The Internet has been the primary cause of the shift in forex markets — from telephone and chat trading to online trading. According to a report released in 2007 by Celent, an international strategy consultant, the use of electronic trading systems accounted for more than 75 percent of the total interbank spot trading in 2006, in contrast to less than 33 percent in 1998. Most electronic trades are handled through two primary electronic platforms, Reuters Dealing and Electronic Broking System (EBS). Reuters, a London based news organization, was one of the first to establish an electronic platform to communicate with the global trading community and has often handled interbank trades for large traders. EBS, established in 1993, is a UK-based foreign exchange provider documented as having 2,000 traders on 750 global dealing floors. The advent of these two electronic platforms made traditional telephone communication obsolete. Many retail platforms have been modeled after the EBS electronic system.

Forex Firms

Most large forex firms trade in the interbank market with banks such as the Hong Kong and Shanghai Banking Corporation (HSBC), Deutsche Bank, or JP Morgan. A trader who uses one of the major global financial institutions is trading in the interbank market, which starts with lots of $1 million. Each forex firm has a market maker who maintains order and provides liquidity in the market through market trade pricing. Forex firms receive price information feeds from outside providers such as EBS, Reuters, or the banks involved in the trades. Market makers review those outside feeds and establish pricing to offer to clients. Each forex firm also has a market specialist who intervenes in market situations when there are temporary price disparities.

Forex Dealers

Forex dealers make trading opportunities available to retail investors by acting as counterparties for forex trades and providing an orderly retail market. Full-service forex dealers handle settlement of transactions, extend credit to investors, and provide a number of other back-office services. The role of the forex dealer is a combination of market maker and market specialist in the equity market. When a retail trader views a quote, a forex dealer provides that quote. Firms that act as forex dealers must register as Futures Commission Merchants (FCMs). The Commodity Futures Trading Community (CFTC), an independent entity of the U.S. government, provides information on all Futures Commission Merchants (FCMs) in its Background Affiliation Status Information Center (BASIC). You can find BASIC on the CFTC website at **www. nfa.futures.org/basicnet**. FCMs are required to file monthly financial reports with the Division of Clearing and Intermediary Oversight, a division of the CFTC, and the information is made public 12 days later.

In the United States, FCMs are the market makers for retail forex. The CFTC and National Futures Association (NFA) implement strict requirements, similar to rules established for dealers and brokers in the securities market, for all FCMs. Requirements include adequate capitalization and specific provisions regarding ethics and protection against fraud.

> ### TIP: Do not trade with a dealer who is not an FCM.
>
> It is illegal for a person or a firm to act as a counterparty in a forex trade unless registered as an FCM or as a Materially Affiliated Person (MAP) of an FCM. (Commodity Futures Modernization Act, Section 4k(1)) A forex dealer who is not registered as an FCM may be operating a scam.

Forex dealers do not trade in the interbank market, though some claim to do so. Forex dealers provide an opportunity for retail traders, who do not have the credit rating or trading volume to trade in interbank, to trade in a limited subset of the larger interbank market. These dealers break some large currency deals into smaller units to sell to individual investors. Retail traders are limited to accepting the price established by the dealer and allowing the dealer to trade on their behalf. Retail quotes closely mirror those of interbank prices provided by forex firms. A forex dealer has no legally binding obligation to provide liquidity or an orderly market in extreme conditions, as forex firms do, a fact documented in the account opening documents of most FCMs.

An introductory broker (IB) is a forex broker who provides technical support and advice but is not a market maker. He or she must rely on an FCM for pricing and trade execution and refer all trade execution and floor operations to an FCM. An IB is client-oriented and typically works with a single FCM, which limits the amount of market depth required of the client and the number of execution options offered to the client. An IB is prohibited from holding any type of funds on behalf of the client and must refer all financial matters to his or her FCM.

Retail forex traders are vulnerable under extreme market conditions because they trade with a single dealer. If a specific dealer is unable to provide executable prices, the trader has no other recourse. In addition, the leverage offered by most retail forex dealers might eventually outpace actual trading activities. A crisis in liquidity occurs if the proportion of buyers to sellers becomes unbalanced.

Retail platforms

The software applications retail forex brokers use to facilitate trades are called platforms. Retail platforms may be either single market-maker platforms or multiple market-maker platforms. Single market-maker platforms allow a trader to trade with a single counterparty on a single quote. Multi market-maker platforms allow a trader to choose with whom to trade and to select from multiple quotes. All platforms are based on three types of trading mechanisms — hub and spoke, request for quote, and click and deal. It is important to understand the advantages and disadvantages of each trading system.

Hub-and-spoke trading

Hub-and-spoke trading is done on platforms that allow multiple market makers to post bids and allow participants to choose their own counterparties. All networked participants may post bids and offers, while seeing the bids and offers of other traders. The mechanism of hub-and-spoke trading provides traders with the closest available view of an entire market. There is no price manipulation or trading desk, creating a transparency that results in greater depth and more competitive pricing. However, hub-and-spoke trading may quickly lead to a liquidity crisis if all the participants trade on one side of a currency pair and there is no taker for the other side of the trade. If a major crisis prompts traders to sell a particular currency, the situation may become critical. The currency will continue to drop in value until a buyer decides to buy.

The mechanism of hub-and-spoke trading is found in many institutional platforms, such as Currenex and FxConnect. One version of hub-and-spoke trading, used by Hotspotfx, CoesFX, and GFTs Inter Trader Exchange, that allows traders to trade directly with one another on the platform, promises to be the future of retail forex trading.

Request-for-quote trading

Traders may request quotes from a market maker using a platform that incorporates a feature similar to instant messaging. The request is usually for a currency pair and trade size, and the response is a two-sided price quote. Request-for-quote trading tends to favor the market maker because only the market maker sees the trade and positions before making a quote. A dealer may then adjust that price up or down before responding to a trader's request for a quote. Request for quote is an older trading mechanism, still used and preferred in most trades in excess of $25 million.

Click-and-deal trading

Click-and-deal trading is the most common type of platform used in retail forex. The advent of the Internet made "what you click is what you get" (WYC/WYG) technology available to online computer users. The click-and-deal mechanism, otherwise known as one-click dealing or executable streaming price feed, provides live quotes that may be traded instantly. Most prices are streamed — they are continually up-dated — providing for an orderly and dependable market. Though there are established limits on the amount that may be traded at a particular price, these limits are high enough to satisfy most retail traders. Click-and-deal trading allows for price transparency and limits the advantage held by market makers in request-for-quote trading. Market makers are required to post two-sided quotes, and traders have the option of deciding whether to trade on the quote before making a commitment. Traders can see the quote price before revealing their intentions to the dealer.

Forex Brokers

Brokers in the forex market get a commission for matching buyers and sellers. An Introducing Broker (IB) or FCM representative fulfills the role of a broker in retail forex trade. An IB must also register with the CFTC. *For more information on U.S. forex brokers see Appendix D.*

Because there is not a centralized location for forex trading, you will need to engage the services of a forex broker to participate in market events. Most brokers may be found online, but some brokers use tradi-tional voice and paper services, or both. The forex market is generally unregulated, but many legitimate brokers are registered with regulatory agencies and should be able to provide traders with documentation and references. There are many safe and reputable forex brokers, but illegiti-mate off-exchange currency dealers and other market scams exist and should be avoided.

Broker policies

Like other business entities, currency brokers have contract agreements that outline the role of each party to the contract. As with any contract, a contract with a currency broker should be carefully examined and thoroughly understood. Read the fine print in a broker's contract and pay particular attention to trading hours, available currency pairs, required transaction costs, rollover charges, margin requirements, margin interest, lot size requirements, and any requirement not fully understood. The following are some of the particulars typically defined in a forex broker contract:

- **Trading hours.** Though most brokers operate on the same time clock used in the global forex market, which is 5 p.m. EST Sunday through 4 p.m. EST Friday, confirm the trading hours of your chosen broker.

- **Currencies traded.** Every broker should trade the seven major currency pairs, but some brokers will not risk trading certain cross currency pairs. Clarify which currencies you will be able to trade on a specific platform.

- **Transaction costs.** Transaction costs are applied to each trade and must be subtracted from any profit you make from trades. Transaction costs are measured in pips — the lower the number of pips, the greater your profit. You can determine transaction costs by comparing pip spreads across brokers, or use a less scientific form of comparison that involves examining the bid/ ask spread of EUR/USD trades — the most traded currency pair in the market. Though a bid/ask spread of 2 pips is preferred, a bid/ask spread that does not exceed 3 or 4 pips is often acceptable. *For more information on pips, see Chapter 4.*

- **Rollover charges.** Rollover charges, which is interest determined by the differential between currencies in a currency pair, increase as the differential between the two currencies increases. Be sure you understand the broker's use of rollover charges and the exact time they are applied. Margin accounts earn interest that fluctuates with a particular country's market rate. Even when no trading activity is being done, the account should continue to earn interest from the party that holds the account.

- **Margin requirements.** A margin requirement is the minimum amount that you must hold in your trading account as a security deposit. When your account balance drops below the minimum requirement, the broker may immediately demand that you deposit additional funds.

- **Lot sizes.** Brokers establish their own lot sizes, as well as mini-lot sizes when applicable. Lot sizes may vary from 1,000 to 100,000 units, and mini-lots are offered at one-tenth of a lot. Brokers offer fractional unit sizes to allow traders a choice of unit size. Clarify the lot sizes available under a broker's contract.

Fraudulent brokers

Between 2004 and 2009, the CFTC's Division of Enforcement filed 238 cases of enforcement action against fraudulent financial companies. Hundreds of firms, owners, and employees have defrauded customers of more than $280 million. Fraudulent firms have been known to offer bid/ask spreads in excess of 30 pips and require commissions of as much as $200 per trade. Many of the guilty parties have been prosecuted and sentenced, but defrauded investors rarely recover the funds they have lost.

The most common fraudulent practices identified by the CFTC are:

- Promising profit that is never delivered

- Claiming that most customers make a profit when, in fact, most of their customers lose money

- Claiming to be trading with customers' funds when they are misappropriating those funds

- Advertising fake success stories or using fake customers

- Providing customers with fake account statements that show false trading profits

- Claiming long tenures in the business when they have only been in business for a matter of months

- Claiming to be a stable and solid firm, and then disappearing with customers' funds and providing customers with no contact information

Broker selection

Finding the right broker is critical to your success in forex. In the absence of a centralized exchange, there is a pool of global forex broker platforms. Choosing a currency broker requires thought and work. Do not simply choose the first broker that looks good or give in to high-pressure sales tactics. Before you commit yourself to trading with a broker, screen your prospects carefully using the following method:

- Select at least three prospects and make a comparative analysis of the three. While speaking to the sales representative, ask if the broker can offer you an even better deal.

- Check the National Futures Association's Background Affiliation Status Information Center (BASIC) (**www.nfa.futures.**

org/basicnet) to confirm that your prospects have not been disciplined or removed from the market. The BASIC database includes names of associated companies and lists the violations perpetrated by defunct and fraudulent companies.

- Ask your prospects for references and contact them.

- Check with the regulatory agency in the country where the broker is located to confirm that a particular broker is regulated.

- Join forex discussion groups on the Internet and ask for information from other investors about their brokers. Brokers and their representatives also participate in these discussion groups and may respond to your inquiries by promoting themselves, so be alert.

- Type each broker's name in an Internet search engine to see if there are any references to the broker in news articles or financial blogs.

- Study how often the brokers requote. The uncentralized nature of the forex market sometimes makes it necessary for a broker to requote the price of a currency after a trader has already accepted a trade. All brokers will requote occasionally, but those who requote often, especially when a trader is winning, should be avoided. Some requoting is expected in fast moving markets, but an excessive number of requotes when traders have big wins is suspect.

- Review your prospective brokers' documentation, which is usually available on their websites. Compare the clarity of the language of the documents.

- Request information from prospects and compare the responses of each prospect. Does the broker respond in a timely and professional manner? What form of communication does the broker offer? Can you correspond with a customer service representative by e-mail or in a live chat session?

- Call any advertised numbers to ensure validity and to determine that the listed contact is accessible and reliable.

- Compare account minimums, margins, pip spreads, account withdrawals, lot fees, and other factors that affect trade profits. Determine if fees and requirements are within market norms. Request hard copies of price lists, requirements, and fee schedules.

- Try out the free demos, paper trades, and mini-accounts offered by prospective brokers to see how easy it is to use their particular platforms and identify potential problems.

- Read other users' opinions and reviews of the chosen platforms on discussion boards.

TIP: Avoid being scammed.

An Internet search for "forex" will pull up thousands of websites. Among the many legitimate brokers and dealers are unscrupulous bucket shops and "brokers" whose business is either to cheat gullible investors or overcharge for services that are much less expensive elsewhere. Be wary of any broker who promises outrageous returns or guarantees profits. Other clues are unprofessional-looking websites and grammatical or spelling errors, which could indicate the owner of the site is based overseas. If you are not trading with a U.S. company you will have little recourse if it goes into bankruptcy or mishandles your transactions. Trade only with dealers and brokers who are registered with the Commodity Futures Trading Commission (CFTC). Do a background check on BASIC (**www.nfa.futures.org/basicnet**). Finally, make sure your dealer is large enough to handle heavy trading during a volatile market, or your orders may not be filled efficiently.

Online Dealer and Broker Services

Traditionally, banks have manipulated the forex market by guarding information, making the price discovery process difficult for outside investors, and ensuring that mistakes by outside investors were costly. Banks were responsible for keeping bid/ask spreads wide and transaction costs high. Advances in computer and Internet technology have made it possible for retail traders to trade online with pricing and execution comparable to that used in the interbank market. The Internet allows the instant, widespread dissemination of information among millions of people worldwide, resulting in less costly trades, easier execution, and finer accuracy in currency pair pricing. A constant flow of orderly quotes is provided to traders, even during volatile periods.

Almost all forex brokers provide an online platform for traders to conduct business. Most platforms are built to run under the MS Windows® operating system and may include JAVA™ extensions or Adobe® Flash® animations.

A good platform offers the following:

- Easy access to the order entry process

- Bar charts of currency pairs being monitored

- Easy access to a listing of currently held positions

- An account summary that includes current account balances, available margins, margins locked in active positions, and realized and unrealized profits and loss

- A voice backup system that allows for traders to conduct business whenever the Internet is not accessible

Online forex platforms vary widely in structure and in the extent at which it can connect directly to the forex market. Before selecting a particular platform, evaluate it carefully. In addition to the platforms of legitimate retail forex brokers, numerous forex scams exist on the Internet. Online forex platforms can be classified as follows:

- **Retail market makers (RMMs)**: The majority of online dealer platforms are retail market makers who give individual traders access to the forex market and profit from the spread in each transaction.

- **Institutional market makers**: These platforms are very closely aligned with the forex interbank market. Investors must meet the required account minimums in order to trade on these platforms.

- **Institutional forex**: This platform is the Intranet-based trading system of Electronic Broking System (EBS), a consortium of nearly 200 banks that account for more than 50 percent of Forex bank trades. Participants must be banks.

- **Bookmakers**: These platforms exist to place bets on currency. Bookmakers are legitimate in some countries.

- **Bucket shops**: These platforms are scams that have no connection to the forex market, except the association they fraudulently claim. The broker itself acts as the counterparty in every trade and never passes the trades on to a bank. That way, it makes money not only from the spread but also from the traders' losses. Typically, bucket shops attempt to lure investors into engaging in currency futures and options rather than spot forex trades, because they can swindle more money from unsuspecting investors.

Opening an online account

There are four steps to opening an online account with a forex broker: select the type of account, complete registration, activate the account, and confirm the account.

1. **Account selection:** Forex brokers offer both individual and corporate online accounts, and may further subdivide these categories based on the amount being invested. Inexperienced traders are encouraged to use spot-market accounts because they are easiest to rollover. Accounts for trading forex derivatives, such as futures and options, are also available. Most of the fraud in forex is attributable to trading schemes in the futures and forwards markets.

2. **Registration:** Brokers establish their own requirements for account registration. Typically, you will be asked to complete an application, submit a W-9 tax form, sign a risk disclosure form, and sign consent to conduct business electronically. These forms are usually available for download on the platform where you are registering.

3. **Activation:** Brokers will provide instructions for activating an account after registration is completed. Usually a credit card is validated for use or an initial deposit is required.

4. **Confirmation:** After an account is activated, a trader's identity is confirmed by the assignment of a username and password necessary to gain access to the account.

---

*TIP: Always have a back-up power supply
and a reliable Internet connection.*

Online trades can be interrupted if a network failure disrupts Internet connections, or if a computer system suddenly shuts down because of a power failure. Most trading platforms have a backup power supply, but your computer should also have a backup. Any persistent Internet disconnection problems should be addressed before beginning online trading. Look for platforms that indicate whether a network connection is established and whether data streams are being collected real time. Computer viruses, hackers, and security threats can also interfere with online trades.

Complimentary services

Many platforms have integrated software products that provide investors with the ability to perform charting and technical analysis. A dealer platform may integrate a software package as part of an upgrade to their software, or partner with another firm that specializes only in the integrated product. The level of integration and compatibility of the integrated products vary from platform to platform. Dealer platforms may also offer bilingual platforms or accounting services to complement their trading services. Most retail platforms include news feeds and commentary to assist in your analyses of the market.

Charting packages

Charting packages are standard with most forex online accounts. A good charting package is necessary to represent historical price data visually, and offers tools that allow you to manipulate the data. Data may be displayed in time increments, by period, by currency pairs, and by a number of technical indicators. Determine the source of the data feeds used to produce the charts in charting packages. Because there is no centralized forex market, data may be derived from any number of sources. No two feeds and subsequent charts will be exactly the same, and one feed is not necessarily better than the other. Data feeds from EBS and Reuters may represent the true market better than other sources, but they are expensive. Most platforms use a single charting system and provide reference to others. For more accurate data representation, invest in additional charting services and compare charts.

News feeds

Advancements in electronic communication have provided quick access to information and news, but many Web-based news broadcasts tend to lag behind the currency market. Market indicators are usually broadcast after the information has spread within the trading community through other means. Because seconds can mean the difference between a loss and a profit, the late broadcast of news feeds might present a disadvantage. Event-driven traders and those who trade on fundamentals should invest in higher level news feeds. Traders who primarily rely on news feeds to provide indicators should combine news feeds with television business news, such as Bloomberg reports.

Help and education

Many online broker platforms offer educational and training services to first-time users. The platform should also include some form of customer service with clearly stated contact information, or at least a help directory and frequently asked questions (FAQ) menu. Platforms offering news services or news feeds on their Web pages provide traders with information they may use in selecting currency pairings and deciding positions. Even though online chats offer an effective way of allowing traders to communicate with each other, the chat rooms provided on many platforms are not reliable. Be wary of unsolicited tips and advice from unknown persons and sources.

Paper trading

Paper trading — a valuable educational tool — is available on many forex platforms. Inexperienced traders can practice with a demo account, trading in a real-time environment, but with no real exchange of money. Demo trades exist only on paper and give traders an opportunity to familiarize themselves with a particular platform and test trading strategies without assuming any risks. Demo accounts are free and serve as a sort of hands-on advertisement and trial of the platform.

TIP: Demo accounts are not the same as live trading.

Demo accounts are offered as enticements to draw inexperienced new-comers into forex trading. They offer a valuable opportunity to practice forex trading before entering the market, and for testing trading strategies. Newcomers are encouraged to do "paper trades" with a demo account until they feel confident to trade with real money. However, demo accounts do not behave exactly like the real forex market. Because orders in a demo account are not real transactions, they are "filled" immediately. Real orders are often subject to price checks and there may be delays and even price requotes before they are filled. There is also a possibility that a large buy or sell order will not be totally filled if a counter-party is not available. There is also a psychological element: An inexperienced trader may not be able to act with the same confidence when real money is at stake, as he or she did when trading with a demo account.

Micro accounts

Some dealers allow traders to establish mini accounts with as little as a $100 deposit. These small accounts are useful to the novice trader in testing trading strategies and skills, but because the profit on each unit of currency is often just a fraction of a cent, larger accounts are necessary to make trading profitable.

Spot Trading

Spot trading in the forex market is called forex. A forex exchange of one currency for another is a simple, simultaneous transaction that can be settled within two days, with the exception of Canadian transactions, which can be settled within one day. The relative simplicity of the spot forex market has been partially responsible for attracting participation in the forex market.

There are two parties to every contract — a short position and a long position. The party who is obligated to deliver a commodity holds the short position. The party who is obligated to receive the delivered commodity holds the long position. As long as there are willing counterparties to a trade and liquidity in the currency pair being traded, there are no restrictions or limitations in forex trading.

Derivatives

Derivatives, which move the market and affect pricing, include futures, forwards, options, and swaps. Many inexperienced forex traders focus on spot trading because of its simplicity and growing popularity. However, a concentrated focus on just one of the established forex trading instruments limits investors' ability to trade effectively. Spot transactions are over-the-counter transactions, handled outside an organized exchange. No single party can keep track of spot activity, because it allows investors to get in and out of the market at will. Trades such as futures and options, which are made through organized exchanges, are managed and documented, and the information is made available to investors. CME Group, the world's largest futures and options exchange, reports all outstanding positions for options on its website (**www.cmegroup.com**). Investors can use this data to predict the future of the market. This type of information is not available for spot transactions.

Forwards trading

A forwards trade is a trade in which the date of delivery for a commodity is established for some time in the future. Typically, a forward contract is made for one, two, three, six, or twelve months. Traders may use forwards to take advantage of interest rate differences between countries. For example, if the U.S. interest rate is established at 5 percent and the European interest rate is established at 8 percent, traders may convert their U.S. dollars into euros to receive the higher interest paid by the European Central Bank (ECB).

In theory, traders may also buy U.S. dollars for some time in the future so they lock in a favorable current exchange rate. When the dollars are delivered at the later date, the trader will theoretically have more dollars left over. In reality, the price of a forward contract may be more expensive (or cheaper) than the current spot price of the currency. Differences in interest rates are factored into the cost of most forward contracts, as established by the market. In the theoretical situation above, the trader is not likely to have more dollars left over, because the market will dictate a more expensive forward contract for euros to account for the superior rate of return. The higher price attached to the forward contract is called a premium. A cheaper price is called a discount. The value of a forward is not determined by the market's anticipation of how much a currency will be worth in the future relative to another currency, but by the difference in interest rates offered by the two countries.

Futures trading

A futures trade is very similar to a forwards trade. A contract binds a buyer and seller in a trade of currency for a predetermined price at some predetermined time in the future. The difference between a futures and forward trade is that future trades are traded on a regulated exchange and forwards are not. The Chicago Mercantile Exchange (CME) was the first to offer futures when it was founded in 1972. A full range of futures is still available at the CME via the GlobeEx trading platform, which makes futures available 24 hours per day.

Trades in the currency futures market incur a round-turn commission — a commission charged on both the purchase and sale of a futures contract — that can vary from broker to broker. In contrast, trades in the currency spot market incur a transaction charge equal to the difference between the current bid price and the ask price for each trade. Investors are typically required to maintain higher margins in the futures market than those required for the forex spot market.

An investor must make a deposit on a futures contract to provide a margin or bond for the trade. If market events suggest a currency will increase in value over the next year, a contract that locks in a lower price will become more valuable. At the end of each business day, the difference between the price for a future and the market price of currency is established. That difference is then added to or subtracted from the margin. Losses to the margin must be replenished for the trader to be able to hold a position in the market.

A futures contract specifies the precise terms and conditions of a trade agreement. A futures contract should include the following components:

- Quality of the commodity
- Quantity of units
- Price per unit
- Date of delivery
- Method of delivery

The price stipulated in the contract is the price that both parties agree will be paid on the future date specified as the date of delivery.

Spot currency trades that cannot be settled within two business days are typically routed through an authorized commodity futures exchange. The International Monetary Market (IMM), a division of the Chicago Mercantile Exchange (CME) that specializes in currency futures, stock index futures, interest-rate futures, and options on futures, is such an exchange.

Contract specifications

The table below shows some typical currencies traded through the IMM and the contract specifications defined by the CME. The contract size represents one contract requirement. Some brokers also offer mini-contracts, which are one-tenth the size of a standard contract. The delivery month's column indicates the months for delivery. The symbols H, M, U, and Z are acronyms representing March, June, September, and December. Trading hours specifies the CME's local trading hours in Chicago. The minimum fluctuation is the smallest monetary unit registered as 1 pip in price movement at the exchange. The minimum fluctuation is usually established as one-ten thousandth of the base currency.

Futures Contract Specifications

Contract	Trading Hours	Delivery Months	Contract Size	Minimum Fluctuation
Australian Dollar	7:20-2:00	H, M, U, Z	100,000 AUD	1 pt=$10.00
British Pound	7:20-2:00	H, M, U, Z	62,500 GBP	2 pts=$12.50
Canadian Dollar	7:20-2:00	H, M, U, Z	100,000 CAD	1 pt=$10.00
Eurodollar	7:20-2:00	H, M, U, Z	$62,500 EUR	1 pt=$25.00
Japanese Yen	7:20-2:00	H, M, U, Z	12,500,000 JPY	1 pt=$12.50
Mexican Peso	8:00-2:00	H, M, U, Z	500,000 MXN	2.5 pts=$12.50
Swiss Franc	7:20-2:00	H, M, U, Z	125,000 CHF	1 pt=$12.50

Commodity Trading Adviser (CTA)

A CTA is an expert in the field of trading commodities and futures contracts who provides investors with advice and strategies. Investors usually develop one-on-one relationships with CTAs, an effective method for learning about forex trading. CTAs must be registered with the National Futures Association (NFA) and are required to pass a Series 3 or a Series 7 examination administered by the Financial Industry Regulatory Authority (FINRA).

Options trading

An option is a currency-trading contract that gives an investor the option to buy a specific amount of currency at an established price (the strike price) on or before a specified date. Options differ from forwards and futures because investors can choose not to exercise the option. Most investors who use options rely on stability in currency exchange rates for business transactions or foreign investments. Options are an effective and relatively cheap tool for hedging against fluctuations in foreign currency. The buyer locks in an exchange rate and uses the option only if the market exchange rate becomes unfavorable.

As with other currency exchanges, options require a seller (sometimes referred to as a writer) and a buyer. The right to buy currency is a call option, and the right to sell currency is a put option. The price for which a buyer agrees to pay or sell currency is called the strike price or exercise price. The amount of currency that can be bought or sold under the option is called the principal. Options have a specific time limit before they expire. In the United States, a buyer may exercise a call option on any business day, including the expiry date. In the European market, a buyer may exercise a call option at any time, but no currency is delivered until the expiry date. In general, less than 20 percent of all options fail to be exercised by the expiry date.

A buyer pays a premium to purchase an option. If the buyer fails to exercise the option, the premium is forfeited. The prices of premiums are set by the market and adjusted according to the market's perception of the likelihood that the option will be exercised. Some premiums are simply the difference between the current spot price and the future strike price. Other premiums use more complex calculations that account for market conditions and the expiry date.

Options may be bought, sold, and re-sold as market conditions warrant, and may be bought on an exchange or over-the-counter. Most exchanges offer U.S. style options and standardize the options, setting a strike price, expiry date, and contract size. The CME is one of the major exchanges that offer standardized and customized currency options. The CME offers its options primarily in currencies with strong economies such as the U.S. dollar, Australian dollar, Canadian dollar, British pound, euro, yen, and the Mexican peso. Options bought over the counter are bought in interbank. Options offered in the interbank market are usually European style options, in which the terms of the contract are negotiated between the seller and buyer.

Swaps

A swap is a combination of a spot trade and a forward trade. A swap agreement between two parties specifies a trade of currency on a specified date and an agreement to trade it back on another date. A swap provides investors with an alternative to borrowing foreign currency. An investor who needs liquidity in a currency may swap for the needed currency. For example, through a spot transaction an investor may trade U.S. dollars for Japanese yen and, by using a forward transaction, the investor also agrees to buy back the dollars in the future. In the meantime, the investor has use of the yen for business or other purposes. Large corporations and other major players in the forex market tend to be the most favorable to swaps, and individual investors rarely use them.

Chapter 4

The Language of Forex

Forex has a terminology of its own. This chapter explains some of the words and phrases used by participants in the forex market. You will need to become familiar with these terms and concepts in order to understand the information given by forex dealers.

Major and Minor Currencies

Major currencies are the seven currencies that experience the highest trading volume. They are: USD, EUR, JPY, GBP, CHF, CAD, and AUD. The six trading pairs that involve major currencies account for about 90 percent of the total forex trade. These are: USD/JPY, USD/CHF, USD/CAN, EUR/USD, GBP/USD, and AUD/USD. All other currencies are considered minor. Of the minor currencies, the NZD, ZAR, and SGD are the three currencies that experience the most trade volume. It is difficult to determine the ranking of other minor currencies because international trade agreements often limit their liquidity.

Currency Pairs

A Forex trade involves the simultaneous buying and selling of two currencies. The two currencies used in the trade are referred to as a currency pair, which is demonstrated as two currencies separated by a slash — for example, USD/GBP. The first currency is the base currency — the currency being bought — and the second currency is the quote currency — the currency being sold.

Quote Conventions

A forex transaction can be quoted in terms of either of the currencies involved in the trade, but the quote must always have two sides. The exchange rate used in the forex market might be expressed as follows:

Base Currency/Quote Currency   Bid Price/Ask Price

For example, the exchange rate for the euro/
U.S. dollar pair might be expressed:

EUR/USD   1.2406/08

The base currency is always equal to one. The quote currency is the amount necessary to purchase one unit of the base currency. The ratio of base currency to the quote currency may be expressed as a single value — the relationship between two currencies. For example, EUR/USD 1.2406 indicates that for every euro, a trader can receive 1.2406 U.S. dollars — the bid price.

If the EUR/USD quote increases from 1.2406 to 1.2606, the euro is strengthening and the dollar is weakening. A decrease from 1.2406 to 1.2296 indicates that the dollar is strengthening and the euro is weakening. If the trend of the dollar shows it is strengthening against the euro, it is more advantageous for a trader to buy USD/EUR, which would be a trade buying U.S. dollars and selling euros. If the market trend indicates a weakening of the dollar, a trader should sell USD/EUR.

In the currency market, market trends can be determined by examining currency pairs over time. Generalizations, such as "the dollar is strong," are used to express historic trends and trading norms. A knowledgeable trader always speaks of the relative position of a currency in a currency pair. For example, "the dollar is strengthening against the euro."

The U.S. dollar is the basis of the global forex market, and is accepted universally as the basis for numerous other currencies. The value of these currencies is typically expressed as the amount necessary to purchase one U.S. dollar. The USD is quoted as their base currency. When USD is quoted as the base currency, the quote is said to be in "European" or "indirect" terms. When another currency is quoted as the base currency, specifically, the euro (EUR), the British pound (GBP), or the Australian dollar (AUD), the quote is in "American" or "direct" terms.

Typically, when a bid price and ask price are being quoted, only the final two digits of the bid price are shown. For example:

EUR/USD   06/08

When the ask price is more than 100 pips above the bid price, three digits will be displayed on the right hand side of the slash — for example, EUR/CZK 32.2456/870. This indicates a weak quote currency.

Base currency

The first currency in a currency pair is referred to as the base currency. A price quote shows how much of the quote currency is needed to sell or purchase one unit of the base currency. USD is normally considered the base currency in the forex market.

Quote currency

The quote currency is the second currency in a currency pair. The quote currency is also referred to as the pip currency. Any unrealized loss or profit is expressed in the quote currency.

Cross currency pairs

Cross currency, or cross rate, is a currency pair that does not include U.S. dollars or the euro. Cross currency pairs effectively equate to two separate currency pairs. A GBP/JPY trade, for example, is equivalent to buying a GBP/USD currency pair and selling a JPY/USD currency pair or buying a GBP/EUR currency pair and selling a JPY/EUR currency pair. As a result, cross currency pairs are likely to carry higher transaction costs than currency pairs that include the U.S. dollar or euro. Currency pairs that include the euro are called euro cross currency pairs. The three most-traded euro cross rates include EUR/JPY, GBP/EUR, and GBP/JPY.

Because the Forex market provides for any nation's currency to be traded against any other nation's currency, there are hundreds of currency pairs in the market. When a cross trade involves one of the more obscure nations, the pairing is called an exotic currency pair and carries a higher liquidity risk — the risk that you will not be able to buy or sell the currency when you want to.

Price Interest Points (pips)

A pip, also referred to as a point, is the smallest unit of price expressed for any traded currency. In the United States, it is the cent. Typically, a currency pair is expressed with five significant digits, and most currency pairs equate to a decimal value with at least one significant figure preceding the decimal point — a currency pair must include at least one unit of currency. The price in a bid/ask price quote is used to establish the number of pips. For example, in the bid/ask quote expressed as EUR/USD 1.2406/08, the price is quoted to four decimal places. As a result, 1 pip is 0.0001 or $1/_{100}$ of a cent. The difference between the bid and ask price is calculated as the absolute value of the two values. For example:

$$| 1.2406 - 1.2408 | = | -.0002 | = 0.0002$$
Because 1 pip = 0.0001 Then 2 pips = 0.0002

In another example, if a bid/ask quote is expressed as USD/JPY 1.06/09, the price is quoted to two decimal places and a single pip is 0.01. The difference between the bid price and ask price is 3 pips.

The value of each pip is calculated by dividing the currency's smallest unit of price by the currency exchange rate. In the EUR/USD example above, if the currency exchange rate of the euro with the dollar is 0.88, the value of each pip is calculated as follows:

$$0.0001 \div 0.88 = 0.000113$$

Ticks

A tick is the smallest interval of time that occurs between two trades of a currency pair. The time intervals between ticks are not uniform. During peak trading periods, there might be multiple ticks during a one-second period for trades on the most active currency pairs, such as EUR/USD or USD/JPY. During non-active periods, there may be two or three hours between ticks for trades with minor cross pairs.

Pips and ticks may be mapped to scale on a graph, with the x-axis representing ticks and the y-axis representing pips, as shown below. These tick charts give a clear picture of the volatility of the currency. The bottom of each bar represents the bid price and the top end the ask price for each trade.

Pips versus Ticks

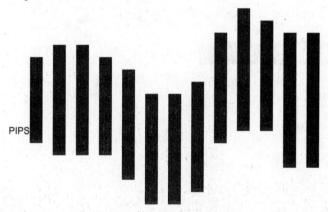

PIPS

TICKS

Margin Account

Each trader is asked to deposit money in a margin account with the forex broker to serve as a security deposit for trades. The minimum amount required for a margin account ranges from as low as $100 to as high as $100,000 and is different from broker to broker. Each time a new trade is executed, a percentage of the margin account balance — calculated based on the currency pair involved in the trade, the currency pair price, and the number of units being traded (lot size) — is allocated to the margin requirement for that trade.

Leverage

Leverage, also referred to as gearing, is the ratio of the amount invested in a trade and the margin required of the currency broker. Leverage is calculated as followed:

100 ÷ the margin percent required by the broker

Leverage varies from broker to broker and may range from 10:1 to 100:1. Leverage allows traders to control relatively large amounts of security with comparatively small amounts of capital. A $500,000 trade leveraged at 100:1 implies that traders need only have 1 percent of the trade value deposited in their broker's margin account.

Trade Value	= $500,000
Leverage = 1:100	= 1 ÷ 100 = 0.01
	= 0.01 X 10
	= 1 %
Margin	= 1% of $500,000
	= 0.01 x $500,000
	= $5,000

The margin gives the trader $500,000 in buying power with a $5,000 deposit.

TIP: Leverage magnifies profit, but it also magnifies risk.

The foreign exchange market is very volatile. Though leverage can increase the buying power of a $5,000 investment to $500,000 — multiplying profit from a trade by 100 — the same buying power can also multiply losses by 100. Be cautious when using leverage to trade.

Margin call

A margin call is a notification from a broker to a trader that his or her margin deposit has fallen below the required minimum because an open trade has moved against the trader. Most online trading platforms automatically calculate profit and loss for open positions each day. Profits are added to the margin account and losses are deducted. If the balance in the margin account sinks below the required minimum, the trader may be required to deposit additional funds into the margin account, or the margin account may be partially or totally liquidated. Some brokers engage in a margin call before liquidation occurs and give traders a two- to five-day window to replenish their accounts; others do not.

TIP: Be sure you understand the terms of your margin account.

Read your broker's contract carefully and have a clear understanding of the terms of your margin account. If an open position suddenly loses value and your margin drops below the required minimum, the broker may close out the position and liquidate your account, locking in the loss. Monitor your account activity on a regular basis, and use stop-loss orders on open positions to limit such risks. *See Chapter 7 for more information.*

Requotes

Sometimes after a trader has placed an order, the broker requotes the price, or even executes the trade at a price higher than the one quoted. Requotes can differ by as much as ten pips from the original price. When markets are fast moving, some requoting is expected; however, some brokers requote arbitrarily when traders are winning to increase their own profit. Requoting is one of the main complaints against online dealers and brokers. Traders who take a loss because of requotes do not have recourse because the broker does not absorb the loss. Technological advances have made requotes less of a problem in stable markets.

TIP: Monitor the pricing on your trading platform.

If requotes occur too often, choose an alternate platform. Look for platforms that offer straight-through processing (STP), in which no time interval elapses between when a trade is placed and the trade is accepted. This type of processing gives dealers no opportunity to manipulate quotes or make order mistakes.

Bid and Ask Price

The bid price of a trade is the price at which the market is prepared to buy a specific currency pair. Traders can sell the base currency at the bid price. The bid price is shown as the first price in a currency pair. The ask price, also referred to as the offer price, is the second price in a currency pair of a trade and indicates the price for which the market is prepared to sell a specific currency pair. Traders can buy the base currency at the ask price. In the quote USD/GBP 1.4536/42, the bid price is 1.4536, which means traders can sell one U.S. dollar for 1.4536 British pounds. The ask price is 1.4542, which means traders can buy one U.S. dollar for 1.4542 British pounds.

Bid/ask spread

The bid/ask spread is the difference between the lower bid price and the higher ask price. The bid and ask prices differ by only a small amount. The spread is expressed in pips and is a function of liquidity and market conditions. The spread is 3 pips on most major currency pairs and 5 pips on all other currency pairs. Currency dealers may express a bid/

ask spread without the inclusion of what is called a big figure quote. A big figure quote includes the first few digits of the exchange rate. In the example USD/GBP 1.4536/1.4542, dealers may quote 36/42 without making reference to the first three digits.

Brokers can manipulate bid/ask spreads to generate more profit for themselves. Every broker receives a commission on currency trades, even those brokers who claim to require "no commission." The broker's commission is usually tied to the bid/ask spread. Instead of charging upfront fees, brokers or futures commission merchants (FCMs) might hide fees in the spread by deliberately increasing the pips for the spread.

Spreads may widen and create volatility in market pricing under certain market conditions. When a central bank decision or monetary decision is made, an unpredicted market event occurs — market conditions become volatile or illiquid; market prices become unstable and volatile.

Lot

A lot is a standardized trading unit of $1,000 leveraged 100:1. A lot gives a trader controlling interest in $100,000 worth of the base currency. Lots have no time restraints or expiration period, because they may be automatically rolled over in trade. Lot size is always expressed as a unit of the base currency. Lot sizes are usually traded for 100,000 even units, but some brokers allow traders to trade in odd lot sizes that are a fraction of 100,000 units.

Mini lot

A mini lot is $1/_{10}$ of a standard lot. A mini lot is a standardized trading unit of $100, also leveraged 100:1. A mini lot gives a trader control of interest in $10,000 worth of a base currency.

Orders

To take a position on a trade, the investor must make an order for the trade. Five types of orders are used in currency trading: market order, limit order, stop order, order cancels others, and stop-limit order.

Market order

A market order is an order to buy and sell currency at the current market price. In the fast-paced forex market, a position to buy or sell may change before an order is carried out, or a position may change because a quote is incorrectly stated. As a result, a market order does not guarantee a quoted price.

Limit order

A limit order prevents an investor from having to buy or sell currency at a higher or lower price than quoted. A buy limit order dictates that currency can only be bought when the price remains at or lower than the limit established by the limit price. A sell limit order dictates that a currency can be sold only at or above the limit price. Some currency brokers charge more to execute a trade with a limit order than they charge for a market order. A limit order that remains active until the end of the day is called a GFD or "good for the day" limit order. A currency dealer will automatically remove a GFD order at the end of the day. A limit order that remains active until the trader cancels the order is called a GTC or a "good 'til canceled" limit order. The trader is responsible for monitoring or canceling a GTC order because the trade dealer will not cancel the order if not instructed to do so.

Stop order

A stop order occurs when a predetermined price automatically triggers a trade. When the predetermined price is reached, a stop order converts to a market order for either purchase or sale. Stop orders may not provide the best return in an unstable market because a brief fluctuation in the wrong direction can trigger an automatic trade, when the overall trend of the market suggests keeping the order active would be best.

TIP: A stop order does not guarantee a price.

A stop order does not guarantee the price that was established when the stop order was converted to a market order. In a rapidly fluctuating market, the market maker may change positions before the execution of a trade is complete. Be sure you understand the established policy regarding stop orders.

Order cancels others

An order cancels others (OCO) is a combination of two limit orders, two stop orders, or a limit order and a stop order. An OCO order allows two orders to be placed with price variables above and below the current market value. When one order is executed, the other order is removed automatically.

Stop-limit order

A stop-limit order is a combination of a stop order and a limit order. When a fast-moving market threatens to trigger a premature stop order, the trader can also place a limit order. A limit order prevents a stop order from being converted to a market order and instead converts the stop order to a limit order. If the price then moves beyond the desired price, the limit order prevents the trade from being executed.

Regulators

No central global entity is responsible for regulating the forex market. Each country has its own form of regulation. Some of the global regulatory authorities include:

National Regulatory Bodies

Country	Organization		Purpose
Australia	ASIC	Australian Securities and Investment Commission	To ensure fairness and transparency of Australia's financial markets, foster investor confidence, and provide education
Canada	IDAC	Investment Dealers Association of Canada	A national self-regulated organization
Hong Kong	SFC	Securities and Futures Commission of Hong Kong	Has jurisdiction over leveraged foreign exchange trading in the city of Hong Kong
Switzerland	SFBC	Swiss Federal Banking Commission	Supervises certain areas of the Swiss financial sector
United Kingdom	FSA	Financial Service Authority of the UK	An independent organization that was given authority to regulate the financial services industry by the Financial Services and Markets Act of 2000
United States	CFTC	Commodity Futures Trading Commission	A government agency with jurisdiction over futures and Forex markets
	NFA	National Futures Association	A non-government, self-regulated organization that issues rules for Forex and futures transactions

Transaction Cost

A transaction cost is the cost for a round-turn trade. A round-turn trade implies both the buy of trade and an offsetting sell or a sell of trade and an offsetting buy of trade of the same size in the same currency pair. Transaction costs are a characteristic of the bid/ask spread and calculated as the ask price minus the bid price. The transaction cost in USD/ GBP 1.4536/1.4542 is 6 pips, calculated as follows:

$$1.4542 - 1.4536 = 0.0006$$
$$\text{Because 1 pip} = 0.0001, \text{6 pips} = 0.0006$$

Rollover

Rollover is the process of rolling an open trade settlement forward to another date. The rollover process incurs a cost based on the interest rate differential of the two currencies in the currency pair. When investors buy currency, they do not actually have the currency deposited into bank accounts — it is reset or rolled over. A rollover allows an investor to hold on to a retail forex position indefinitely.

The international trading day begins at 5 p.m., New York time (EST), when the market opens in Singapore. All retail forex platforms automatically rollover open positions to the next settlement date. The exact time of other rollovers is dependent on the trading platform, and each platform is different; but most rollovers occur daily at 5 p.m. EST. If a trade is made at 5 a.m., London time, the trade will be rolled over at 5 p.m. EST and continue each day for as long as the position is open at 4:59 p.m. EST.

The balance in an investor's trading account may fluctuate because of the interest payments required for open trades. Positions that are open at 5 p.m. EST incur a rollover cost, which is an interest payment that is either paid from or applied to the position, depending on the margin level, currency pair, and the interest rate differential. If the position is closed by 5 p.m. on the next day, no rollover occurs and no interest is paid or applied to the position. A rollover allows investors to maintain their positions without being required to have the currency deposited into their accounts or their positions withdrawn from a trade prematurely.

If a trade's deadline is a weekend away, a trader has a three-day rollover. Interest is calculated as the sum of interest for three days and added or withdrawn from an account on Wednesday at 5 p.m. EST. The three-day rollover offsets trades that would occur on the weekend, had the market been open.

Interest Rate Differential

Interest rate differential is the interest charged for a rollover. The amount of interest charged is dependent on the currency being traded. Because a trader lends in one currency and borrows in another, the trader's account receives interest at one currency's rate and pays interest at another currency's interest rate. Interest rates are established from overnight lending rates set by London Interbank Offered Rates (LIBOR) or a derivative of such rates. For this reason, central banks are important to currency markets.

For example, the prime interest rate established by the Federal Reserve Bank is 2 percent, the rate set by the Bank of England is 4 percent, and the respective LIBOR rates are the same. The spread between the GBP/USD trades is large. A trader would receive 2 percent of total amount traded as long as the margin remains at 2 percent or greater.

TIP: Traders with longer-term positions must watch the interest rate differential.

For most short-term forex trades, the interest rate differential is of no consequence because most trades will exit the market before a rollover takes place. For longer-term positions, the interest rate and its precise application should be carefully weighed against the potential for profit or loss.

Arbitrage

Arbitrage is the purchase or sale of a currency while simultaneously taking the opposite position in a related market, in an attempt to take advantage of small price differentials in the two different markets. Arbitrage is most prevalent when currency prices are out of sync with each other. There are many forms of arbitrage involving multiple markets, currencies, options, and other derivatives. As a simplified example of a two-currency, two-market arbitrage — Bank X offers USD/JPY 200 and Bank Y offers USD/JPY 180. Making use of arbitrage, a trader buys 200 yen for $1 at Bank X. The trader then sells those 200 yen for $1.11 at Bank Y. If the exchange rates remain the same and the trader repeats the transaction, the trader earns a profit as follows:

Two-Currency, Two-Market Arbitrage

Bank X	Cost	Bank Y	Return	Profit
Purchase 200 yen	$1.00	Sell 200 yen	$1.11	11¢
Purchase 222 yen	$1.11	Sell 222 yen	$1.23	23¢
Purchase 246 yen	$1.23	Sell 246 yen	$1.37	37¢
Purchase 274 yen	$1.37	Sell 274 yen	$1.55	55¢
Purchase 305 yen	$1.55	Sell 305 yen	$1.69	69¢
Purchase 339 yen	$1.69	Sell 339 yen	$1.88	88¢
Purchase 376 yen	$1.88	Sell 376 yen	$2.09	$1.09

After seven transactions, the trader has more than doubled the $1 initial investment.

Triangular arbitrage is a forex trading strategy involving buying and selling three currency pairs to take advantage of discrepancies in their prices. For example, suppose you have US $1 million to trade. At a given moment, three currency pairs are priced as follows:

EUR/USD = 0.8550 EUR/GBP = 1. 2800 USD/GBP = 1.546

Almost simultaneously you:

Sell US$1 million and buy 855,000 euros ($1 million x 0.8550)
Sell 854,100 euros for 667,968.8 British pounds (855,100/1. 2800)
Sell 667,968.8 British pounds for US$1,032,680 (667,968.8*1.546)
US$1,032,680 - US$1,000,000 = $32,680 profit

Opportunities for triangular arbitrage do not occur often and typically last for only a few seconds, so this kind of arbitrage requires sophisticated computer equipment or automated trading software.

Intervention

The value of a nation's currency is volatile because it is affected by a number of economic and political conditions. The most notable influences on currency values include interest rates, inflation, political stability, market orders, and international trade. Governments may attempt to influence the value of their currency by flooding the foreign exchange market with their domestic currency to lower the price. They may also buy a significant share of their domestic currency to raise the price. Government intervention in the foreign exchange market to influence pricing is known as central bank intervention. However, the volume and size of the forex market prevents central bank intervention or any other factors from driving the market for any substantial period of time.

Chapter 5

Fundamental Analysis

Fundamental analysis is the study of the core, underlying elements that affect the value of a particular currency. Fundamental analysis attempts to predict price action and market trends by analyzing underlying elements within the framework of business activities and business cycles. Underlying elements include, but are not limited to, economic indicators, social factors, and government policy. Fundamental analyses provide a mechanism to describe how market conditions came to be and predict what price to expect at what time in the future. Fundamental analysis is an effective forecasting tool, but it does not predict exact market prices. After using fundamental analyses to gain a broad picture of the general health of the economy, traders must develop a method for interpreting the information to establish specific entry and exit points, or prices, for currency trades.

Fundamental analysis examines the economic, social, and political forces that drive a nation. Though there are theories suggesting how currencies should be valued, there are no established rules to guide the analysis. Traders must evaluate various macroeconomic indicators, such as inflation, budget deficits, trade deficits, unemployment, and growth rates. Fundamental analysis involves understanding how various reports, announcements, and events move markets. Even though market reaction is unpredictable, most skilled investors can deduce how the market will react under certain circumstances. Traders evaluate macroeconomic data as well as the stability of the government and its established economic policies. The impact of the factors varies from one nation to another. The impact of an event in one nation must be compared against the impact of that event on other nations. Currency trading involves at least two currencies, and the weakening of one nation's economy implies that all currency pairs that share the particular currency will trade lower. Prices are determined by the effect of a weakening or strengthening economy on a particular nation's situation and currency.

Currency movements are not mechanical reactions to events. A skilled currency trader understands how events, particularly unexpected events, affect the global trade market and his or her position in the market. Information is the key to analyzing events, but the importance of that information is subjective. Various interpretations of the same information are responsible for creating volatility in the market. Market behavior, market psychology, predictions of fundamental changes, perceptions, and historical data are all factors in fundamental trading strategies.

TIP: The difficulty of fundamental analysis causes many traders to rely on technical analysis instead.

Fundamental analyses can be stressful for currency traders because this type of analysis does not provide specific entry and exit points, making it difficult for traders to control risks in leveraging techniques. The complexity is often the driving force that prompts some traders to engage in more technical analysis. *For more information on technical analysis, see Chapter 6.*

Fundamental analyses of the currency market include an examination of old news and fresh news. Old news is likely to already be reflected in forex pricing, while fresh news is expected to move markets. Fresh news is any unforeseen event that cannot possibly be factored into current pricing. Fresh news may also result from prescheduled economic events and other prescheduled events, such as news conferences, interviews, and speeches — for example, announcements regarding economic and monetary policy. A single event, such as an announcement of higher interest rates, can have the effect of moving the market up or down and may provide an excellent trading opportunity if properly evaluated. Fresh news will have the greatest impact on markets when such news is combined with a technical analysis of market conditions.

A fundamental trading strategy — news straddle — is used when the outcome of an event is unknown, but it is known that a noticeable market reaction often occurs as a result of the event. Just before or just after the event, traders place trades on both sides of an associated currency pair, near the current price. They then apply technical analysis to determine where to place orders, exits, and stops. This tactic captures a temporary volatility in the market as the market digests new information. Very experienced and educated traders are able to make the most of this strategy.

Supply and Demand

To evaluate economies in a fundamental analysis, it is necessary to understand the supply and demand that drives currency trading. It is assumed that the economic processes that affect supply and demand of currencies can be predicted and observed. The relationship between economic indicators and the evolution of exchange rates must be evaluated. A fundamental currency trading strategy incorporates a strategic assessment of the currency's tradability based on virtually any criteria except price including monetary policy, economic stability, and other fundamentals of a nation's economy.

The health of an economy is reflected in economic indicators, such as trade balance, gross domestic product, and foreign investment. These indicators are responsible for changes in supply and demand for a currency, and currency pricing reflects the balance of supply and demand. The data that supports most economic indicators is released at regular intervals by government or other sources. Of all the available data, interest rates and foreign trade data are most closely analyzed.

Rates of Interest

Changes in interest rates directly impact the currency markets. The market typically reacts favorably when interest rates are lowered, as well as when interest rates are raised because of fears that a national economy is becoming unstable. Some central banks have the authority to attempt to control their nation's money supply by raising or lowering interest rates. Lowering rates makes it cheaper for businesses and consumers to borrow money, stimulating economic growth and consumer consumption. Typically, when interest rates are raised, a nation's currency strengthens in relation to other currencies. On the other hand, when interest rates are raised, many investors withdraw money from the stock market, weakening a nation's currency. Currency traders must figure out which effect will prevail. Often there is a consensus in the market about the effect an interest move will have on a national currency, based on a fundamental analysis of the consumer price index, producer price index, and the gross domestic product. The timing of interest rate moves is also significant and is usually known in advance, because these moves are normally implemented following regularly scheduled meetings of central banks.

Purchasing Power Parity

Purchasing Power Parity (PPP) is the theory that the exchange rates between two currencies are in equilibrium when the purchasing power of the currency is the same in each nation. The theory implies that the exchange rate between two nations should be equal to the ratio of price levels for a fixed basket of goods and services in each country. When a nation experiences inflation, domestic price levels increase, and its exchange rate must then depreciate to achieve PPP.

The law of one price is the basis of PPP. The law of one price states that, excluding transaction costs, natural market competition ensures that the prices of identical goods will be the same in two nations when those prices are expressed in terms of the same currency. For example, the exchange rate for USD/CAD is $1.50. According to the law of one price, a camera bought in the United States for U.S. $200 should cost $300 Canadian dollars in Canada. If the camera can be purchased for less than $300 Canadian dollars in Canada, it would be cheaper, excluding transportation costs, to purchase the camera in Canada than to purchase it in the United States. If large numbers of Americans began purchasing cameras from Canada, such sales would increase the value of the Canadian dollar and make Canadian goods more costly for Americans with U.S. dollars. The U.S. $200 price tag would then seem more reasonable to American consumers, and sales of cameras in America would increase. The law of one price dictates that this process will continue until the two prices reach equilibrium.

The law of one price establishes the following:

- Transaction costs, barriers to trade, and other transaction costs can be significant.

- Competitive markets for goods and services must exist in both nations.

- The law only applies to goods and services traded between nations. Immobile or local goods and services such as homes and land are not tradable.

There are two versions of PPP — absolute and relative. Absolute PPP is based on the equalization of price levels across nations as described above. As an example, the exchange rate between Canada and the United States is calculated as follows:

Exchange CAD/USD = the price level in Canada / the price level in the United States

The PPP exchange rate requires a price level of 1.5 CAD per single USD. The current exchange rate, however, is 0.982 CAD per single USD. The absolute PPP theory dictates that the CAD will appreciate against the USD and, in return, the USD will depreciate against the CAD until equilibrium is reached.

Relative PPP is based on the rate of change of price levels, otherwise known as the inflation rate. The rate of appreciation of a currency is equal to the difference in inflation rates between two currencies. As an example, Canada has an inflation rate of 2 percent, while the United States has an inflation rate of 4 percent. The U.S. dollar will depreciate against the Canadian dollar by 2 percent per year, a theory that holds well when inflation rate differences are large.

One of the simplest methods of measuring PPP between two nations is to compare the price of a standard good, which is identical in both nations. PPP may be measured using a single good as the standard, such as that used in the Big Mac Index, or more sophisticated measurements that look at a basket of goods and services. The problem with the latter is people in different nations tend to consume varying amounts of the same goods and services, making it difficult to compute a truly comprehensive PPP.

Big Mac index

The Big Mac index is a comparison of the price of a McDonald's Big Mac sandwich in different countries. It is used to determine if a currency is undervalued or overvalued. If a Big Mac costs $2 in New York and one euro in Spain, the currency exchange rate should be EUR/USD = 2, so 1 euro = 2 dollars. If a trade is executed at EUR/USD 1.5 (1.5 dollars = 1 euro), the dollar is considered overvalued and the euro is considered undervalued. The theory of PPP then predicts that the dollar will weaken and the euro will strengthen to make up the difference.

Balance of Trade

A nation's balance of trade is the most relied on set of figures used in determining the value of a nation's currency. Balance of trade is a measure of the net difference between imports and exports, as measured over time.

A trade balance deficit exists when the value of imports exceeds the value of exports. Nations that experience regular trade deficits can expect their currency to fall, because a nation's currency is reconverted as it flows into other countries. If more of a currency is sold than bought, then that currency will fall in value. A trade balance surplus exists when the value of exports exceeds the value of imports. Nations with regular trade surpluses can expect their currency to rise in value. When a nation experiences a surplus, more currency is sought than is available, and the demand pushes up the value of the currency.

In reality, the effect of the balance of trade on currency values is not clear-cut. A trade deficit will only cause a currency to fall if the deficit is greater than expectations. For example, a country may experience a trade deficit because the country is successful in attracting foreign capital for investment purposes. The currency value rises temporarily, but investors may then hold back because of skepticism over how long the trend will continue. The theory is represented by the J Curve effect, which is shown in the chart below:

J Curve Effect

A – Current Overall BoP

B - Short-term effect of currency depreciation on BoP

C - Long-term effect of currency depreciation on BoP

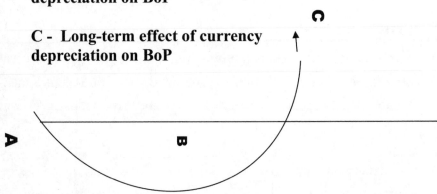

Point A indicates the current balance of trade or balance of payments (BoP), an initial depreciation of currency, and a fall in the currency exchange rate. The depreciation does nothing to improve exports or the trade deficit. In fact, the depreciation increases the amount of currency necessary to purchase imports already obligated for purchase, because changes in the currency exchange rate over time cannot be applied to contracts that have already been signed. In addition, spending on imports rises. As a result, the movement from Point A to Point B indicates that over the short term, an increased trade deficit is experienced to pay for contractually obligated imports. Earnings from exports are not likely to be enough to compensate for the higher spending on imports. However, the movement from Point B to Point C indicates that the balance of trade will improve over the long term as the demand for exports increases and as consumers increase the purchase of domestic goods and services.

Gross Domestic Product (GDP)

The gross domestic product (GDP) is a measure of all economic activity in an economy. The GDP represents the total market value of all goods and services produced by both domestic and foreign companies within a nation's borders. The GDP is a broad measure of economic growth, which should range between 3 percent and 5 percent for advanced industrialized nations such as the United States, Europe, or Japan. A growth rate of less than 3 percent indicates that an economy is stalling, and a growth rate in excess of 5 percent indicates that an economy is in danger of inflation or a crash. It is not uncommon for developing countries to experience much higher growth rates, but too much growth can cause a fall and create interest rate hikes. Most governments release the percentage of growth in GDP on a quarterly basis.

The GDP of differing nations may be compared by either of the following methods:

- Converting the currency value according to the prevailing exchange rates on international currency markets.

- Converting the PPP of each currency relative to a second selected currency, usually USD.

The relative ranking of nations based on their GDP may differ depending on the approach used for conversion. Nations with less developed economies usually have weak local currencies in comparison to world markets. In less developed economies, the use of official exchange rates may understate the relative effective domestic purchasing power of an average producer or consumer by 50 percent to 60 percent. Though calculations based on official exchange rates may provide misleading indicators for domestic measures, a comparison of GDPs, based on official exchange rates does provide an indication of a nation's purchasing power on the international market. To understand how economic data affects currencies, it is necessary to understand the economic characteristics of those markets with the most-traded currencies.

News, whether acquired through the media or government entities, is the primary source of economic data that traders and other market participants use in decision making. News and information provide expectations of the market, which are derived from economic indicators. A trader must differentiate between expected data (or news) and actual data in order to interpret information properly and analyze the impact on markets. The forex market often moves in advance of a data release or news announcement, based on what traders anticipate the news will be. This phenomenon is known as the market discount mechanism. When it is actually released, news that fulfills traders' expectations will have less of an impact on the currency market than unexpected news. The correlation between a currency market and market news is important in determining currency movements.

Specific economic indicators become important in analyzing certain markets. Economic indicators of the major trading markets are of such importance that these should be understood, sought, and analyzed by all market participants. Important economic indicators for seven markets with the greatest trading volume are summarized below. Those seven markets include the United States, Europe, Japan, Great Britain, Switzerland, Canada, and Australia and New Zealand. *For more information on the important economic indicators for each of these nations, see Appendix G.*

Forecasting

Fundamental analysis usually leads to the development of forecasting models, used to formulate trading strategies. Such models draw from various empirical databases and attempt to forecast market behavior and estimate future prices using economic indicators established from historical market data. The forecasts are then used to derive those trades that best exploit the information. Each forecasting model is based on a particular trader's interpretation of the market data, and because each person's interpretation of the same information differs, there are many different forecasting models in use. Traders cannot simply adapt an established model. Each trader must study the fundamentals and determine how the analysis fits into his or her style and expectations.

In forecasting models, the data that composes various economic indicators is not as important as whether the data falls within expectations for a particular market. Traders need to know not only what economic data is released and when, but also the forecast for each indicator in the market. For example, the consequence of an increase in the PPI is not as important for short-term trading as knowing what the market was expecting for the month. If the market predicted a drop in the PPI but instead an increase occurred, the increase may lead to inflation over the long term. A short-term trader can take advantage of the unexpected rise.

Traders need to know what a market is forecasting for various economic indicators and also the key aspects of each indicator. Though unemployment is the headline for the employment index, skilled traders know they should concentrate on non-farm employment data because farm employment data is volatile. Similarly, producer price is the headline figure for PPI, but skilled traders know they will arrive at a more accurate measure of changes in the PPI by excluding changes in food and energy prices because the food and energy components of PPI are very volatile.

Occasionally, economic indicators that have already been published and released are modified. Sometimes an economic indicator falls outside market forecast expectations because the indicator was reported incorrectly. When this happens, revisions to previously released indicators are published with the next scheduled release.

TIP: Changes in the current month's reported data may be due to revisions.

Changes in the current month's reported data may be due to new market actions as well as revisions to previously reported data. Traders must be aware of current and past market conditions to determine which is the case. Be cautious when trading based on economic indicators that fall outside of market expectations because those indicators may be revised in the future.

Economic Indicators

Fundamental analysis incorporates all of the elements that influence a national economy, including government policy, erratic behaviors, and unforeseen events. It is more advantageous for traders, particularly inexperienced traders, to analyze only those elements that have the greatest influence on an economy, instead of attempting to analyze all of the elements. Economic indicators are economic measurements that affect market prices either directly or indirectly. They are compiled and published on a regular schedule to assist market observers in monitoring the state of the economy. Some of the most important U.S. economic indicators include the gross domestic product (GDP), producer price index (PPI), consumer price index (CPI), industrial production (IP), durable goods, employment cost index, retail sales, and housing starts. These statistics summarize the economic data published by various private and government entities and have the potential to generate volume and move market prices.

Economic indicators can be divided into two groups — lagging and leading indicators. Lagging indicators are economic elements that change after an economy has already begun to follow a particular trend or pattern. Leading indicators are economic elements that change before an economy begins to follows a particular trend or pattern and are used to predict changes in an economy.

Traders who analyze economic indicators follow a few simple guidelines to track and organize the data, and then make trading decisions based on the information. It is important to know exactly when economic information will be made public. Schedules of release dates can be on websites such as Econoday (**http://mam.econoday.com**) or acquired from companies that execute trades. The New York Federal Reserve website (**www.newyorkfed.org**) offers charts of global economic indicators. Keeping track of release dates also helps in understanding unanticipated price and market actions. Prices may be directly affected following a public release of data or may be indirectly affected as traders adjust their positions in anticipation of, or in response to, the data.

Understanding which economic indicators reflect what particular aspects of the economy requires some skill and practice in analyzing the data. The GDP, for example, is an indicator of the growth of the U.S. economy, not inflation. Inflation is measured by looking at changes in the consumer price (CPI), producer price (PPI), and employment indices. Some indicators have more potential for moving markets than others. The state of the economy must be considered in determining an indicator's potential for moving markets. If economic growth, not inflation, is a crucial issue for a nation, markets may not react as quickly or dramatically to changes in inflation data. However, changes in the GDP will be anticipated and could create volatility in the market when the news is released.

Some investors rely on data compiled and published in the *Summary of Commentary on Current Economic Conditions,* known as the "beige book," as an indicator of the direction of the U.S. economy. Eight times a year, Federal Reserve Banks in 12 districts gather anecdotal information on current economic conditions through reports from bank directors and interviews with key business contacts, economists, market experts, and other sources, and publish the results in the beige book. The book includes data on consumer spending, manufacturing, real estate, new home construction, wages, and employment. If information in the beige book signals a potential problem, such as inflation, the Federal Reserve Bank responds by taking action. The beige book and other indicators published in the United States are useful for U.S. trading strategies, but the forex market is global. Many countries publish economic data, but they may not be as efficient as the G8 in releasing their information to the public. Research the specifics of any foreign currency you wish to trade. Not all indicators are measured in the same way; some indicators have more weight in the market and not all of them are considered to be accurate.

Governments typically spend more money than they take in. This is not necessarily a bad thing, particularly when the economy is in a recession. The U.S. government distributes money through social programs, such as welfare, Social Security, unemployment insurance, and disability; security and defense contracts; and for emergency situations, such as natural disasters and terrorist acts. Money distributed by the government for these purposes goes into the economy and helps prevent a downward spiral that might lead to economic depression. Economic depression occurs when orders for goods and services fall off and companies reduce their workforces. The workers then reduce their consumption of goods, resulting in an escalating cycle of further reductions in orders, increased layoffs, and reduced consumption. However, the distribution of money by a government is not always an efficient method of allocating resources. For example, governments that hand out contracts to those constituents who will ensure their reelection, or to relatives and friends of government officials, might waste money on ill-conceived projects that do little to support economic growth. The market might react favorably to the election victory of a political party that promises tax relief, but if the tax cuts are then perceived as reckless, the market will fluctuate.

Politics are specific to each nation. A government's attitude and stability are essential to the strength of its currency. Some national leaders might implement processes that are favorable to their own country but damage their country's standing in the international market. Leaders who implement expensive social policy create barriers to free trade, or default on international loans, are considered anti-market. Some investors prefer to invest in nations that allow the market to rule rather than the government, theorizing that stability in currency pricing occurs when costs, services, and trade are naturally brought into balance through markets.

A country's social and political environment also affects the country's currency in ways that are sometimes obvious, and other times almost impossible to recognize. The economic policy of a nation can be subdivided into its monetary policies and its fiscal policies. Monetary policies govern money supply, interest rates, and activities of the central bank. Fiscal policies determine government spending and taxation, while attempting to direct the economy. Monetary policies define how much control a government exerts over its currency. A currency that is heavily controlled by government, such as the Chinese renbi, is called managed currency.

Economic indicators are only one important method of measuring the health of an economy. A nation's social environment is also critical to forex and creates the most volatility in market risks. Significant social events, such as wars, revolutions, and the signing of peace treaties, have a direct effect on markets. Foreign markets offer both the greatest potential for profit and the greatest risks. As a result of social change, factors other than economic indicators can move international pricing, making some markets more or less profitable than others.

The economic health of a country is priced in its currency. To understand price movements of foreign currencies, it is necessary to monitor the specifics of each country's economy.

U.S. economic indicators

U.S. economic indicators are important in understanding the U.S. dollar. The United States is a service-oriented nation, making indicators that describe the service sector particularly significant. Manufacturing accounts for only a small percentage of output, but the large size of the U.S. manufacturing sector makes the U.S. dollar sensitive to any developments in this sector as well. The Fed differs from other central banks in its mandate to control price stability and sustain economic growth. The Fed uses monetary policy to achieve its goal of limiting unemployment, limiting inflation, and achieving balanced growth.

Monetary policy is controlled through federal fund rates and open market operations, including the purchase of government securities such as Treasury notes, bills, and bonds. Such purchases are a signal that policy change will be implemented. An increase in the purchase of government securities typically signals a decrease in interest rates, while the selling of securities signals an increase in interest rates. The federal fund rate is the interest rate that the Fed charges to member banks. The Fed increases this rate to reduce inflation and decreases it to promote growth and consumption. The U.S. dollar is the most traded currency in the world, and it has several important characteristics and economic indicators that are closely watched in the currency market.

U.S. Gross Domestic Product (GDP)

The United States has experienced the highest gross domestic product in the world. About 80 percent of the U.S. GDP results from finance, real estate, transportation, health care, and business services. The estimate of the U.S. GDP for 2009 was about $14.26 trillion. U.S. output was almost three times that of Japan, almost four times that of Germany, and more than five times that of the United Kingdom. Foreign investors consistently increase the purchase of U.S. assets because the United States offers the most liquid equity and fixed income markets in the world. The IMF indicates that foreign investments in the United States are about 40 percent of the total global net inflows into the United States. The United States absorbs about 71 percent of net foreign savings. Should foreign investors decide in large numbers to invest or sell U.S. asset holdings in return for higher yielding assets elsewhere, it would create a significant decline in the value of U.S. assets and the U.S. dollar.

The import and export volume of the United States represents about 12 percent of the U.S. GDP. Though this volume accounts for a small percentage of the overall GDP, the United States has the greatest volume of imports and exports in the world, due primarily to the sheer size of its population. Despite the large amount of import and export activity, the United States also maintains a very large budget deficit, which has been problematic for the economy. Foreign funding of this deficit has been weakening, because many foreign central banks have considered diversifying their reserve assets from U.S. dollars to euros. As a result, the United States has become more sensitive to changes in money flow. To prevent any further decline in the U.S. dollar, the United States needs to attract a significant amount of inflow. In 2009, the United States was in need of an inflow of $40 billion per day to offset the existing deficit.

The United States is also the largest trading partner for many other countries. Foreign trade with the United States accounts for 20 percent of the world's overall trade. The volatility and fluctuation in value of the U.S. dollar affects foreign trade. A weakened dollar could boost U.S. exports, while a strengthened dollar could curb demand for U.S. exports.

The United States' most important trading partners include those nations whose growth and political stability have the biggest impact on the U.S. dollar. Leading U.S. export markets are Canada, Mexico, China, Japan, and the United Kingdom. Leading import markets are China, Canada, Mexico, Japan, and Germany.

The U.S. Bureau of Economic Analysis (BEA) provides two measures of the GDP. One measure is based on income, and the other measure is based on expenditures. The advance release of GDP, published following each quarter of the year, is the most important release of GDP. It includes BEA estimates for data not previously released, trade balances, and inventories. Other GDP releases are considered less significant unless some major revision of the data is included.

U.S. Producer Price Index (PPI)

The PPI measures price changes in the manufacturing sector. The PPI measures the average change in the prices at which domestic producers in manufacturing, agriculture, forestry, electric utilities, natural gas, mining, and fisheries sell their goods. The PPIs used most often in U.S. economic analysis are measures for crude, intermediate, and finished goods. Foreign exchange markets tend to focus on the PPI of seasonally adjusted finished goods and the monthly, quarterly, semi-annual, and annual changes.

Consumer Price Index (CPI)

The CPI measures the average price paid by urban consumers, who account for 80 percent of the U.S. population, for a fixed basket of goods and services. The CPI excludes volatile food and energy components of

consumer spending, but also includes taxes and user fees directly associated with specific goods and services. Price changes are measured in
more than 200 categories of goods and services. The CPI is a key gauge
of inflation and is responsible for driving flurries of activity in the forex
market.

Industrial Production (IP)

IP is a measure of the change in production for a nation's factories, utilities, and mines. IP is a chain-weighted measure — an index provided by
industry type and market type. Referred to as capacity utilization, IP is a
measure of industrial capacity and available industrial resources. Manufacturing accounts for 11 percent of the U.S. economy, and the IP rate
indicates how much of the nation's industrial capacity is in use. Measured increases in the IP index are usually positive for the U.S. dollar.

Institute for Supply Management (ISM) Index

The ISM compiles a monthly composite index that describes manufacturing activity. The index is based on surveys of 300 nationwide purchasing managers in 20 different industries. Calculated ISM index values above 50 are indicators of an expanding economy, and values below
50 indicate a contracting economy.

Durable goods and services

Durable goods and services are measures of new orders placed with domestic manufacturers for immediate and future delivery. A durable good
is a good that lasts at least three years. A durable service is a service that
extends for three years.

Consumer confidence

Consumer confidence is measured by a survey of individual U.S. households. A questionnaire is sent to a representative sample of 5,000 house-

holds nationwide, though it is estimated that only about 3,500 households actually respond to the survey. Each of the chosen households is requested to respond to five questions relative to the performance of the economy. The questionnaire asks households to rate business conditions in their local area during a six-month period, along with job availability and family income. Responses are then seasonally adjusted with an index applied to each response. A composite index is created from the individual indexes. Markets perceive rising consumer confidence as an indicator of higher consumer spending, which indicates possible rising inflation.

Employment Cost Index (ECI)

The U.S. Employment Cost Index (ECI) is an estimated measure of the number of jobs in more than 500 industries in 50 states and 255 metropolitan areas. The estimate considers the number of employees working full-time and part-time in the nation's larger businesses and government. Estimates are acquired through surveys of employer payrolls compiled in the third month of a quarter for the pay period that ends on the twelfth day of that month. The ECI includes wages as well as nonwage costs of employment, which may add as much as 30 percent to the total labor cost.

Employment figures provide an indicator of economic strength because a strong economy creates new jobs. However, if an economy is strong or growing strong, and there are not enough people to fill vacancies, companies compete for the best workers and offer higher salaries. Doing so may hurt the economy, because rapidly rising wages create inflation, which may compel the Fed to raise interest rates to cool the economy. As a result, the job market decreases. Likewise, a weak or weakening economy that is unable to create new jobs indicates uncertainty and decreases consumption, which in turn stalls economic growth. The weak economy may prompt the central bank to lower interest rates, creating economic growth. As a result, high unemployment tends to stimulate the market and low unemployment depresses the market. Overall, the U.S. ECI is generally stable causing very little market reaction.

Non-farm employment

Monthly U.S. employment figures are compiled from data taken from two surveys — the Household Survey and the Establishment Survey. The Household Survey provides data for household employment, the labor force, and unemployment rate. The Establishment Survey provides data from non-farm payrolls, the average hourly workweek, and an aggregate-hour index. Currency traders tend to focus on seasonally adjusted employment and any change in non-farm payrolls. The non-farm sector of employment is the most important and widely watched indicator. Its effect on the forex market is due primarily to political influences rather than economics, because the Fed is always under pressure to keep unemployment under control. Interest rate policy is directly influenced by employment conditions.

Retail Sales Index (RSI)

The Retail Sales Index (RSI) is an estimate of retailers' total monthly sales. The estimate includes samplings taken from retail stores of all kinds and sizes located throughout the nation. Retail sales include the sale of both durable and non-durable goods and services. It includes any excise tax incidental to such sales and excludes any assessed sales tax. RSI is a measure of consumer activity and consumer confidence. Retail sales provide a timely indicator of broad consumer spending patterns, but they can be volatile. As a result, they are adjusted for holidays, trading day differences, and seasonal variations. One of the most important sales figures is past auto sales, because auto sales may vary from month to month.

Housing starts

Housing starts is an estimate of the number of residential properties for which construction has begun. A housing start is the beginning of excavation for the foundation of a property. Housing starts primarily include residential properties. Housing is one of the market sectors most sensitive to interest rates, and one of the first sectors to react to interest rate changes. Any significant housing market reaction to interest rates indicates whether interest rates are nearing a peak or trough. Housing starts are counted and reported monthly, usually near the middle of the month after an estimate has been published. An analysis of housing starts measures the change in levels from month to month.

Balance of international trade

The balance of trade measures the difference between imports and exports of trade in goods and services. Data is provided for total U.S. trade with all countries, detailed information on trade with specific countries and regions of the world, and information on individual commodities. Trade data examined on a monthly basis has proven to be unreliable, so most traders tend to focus on seasonally adjusted trades, measured during a three-month period.

Treasury international capital flow data

TIC flow data is a measure of the monthly capital inflow into the United States — an indicator used in assessing funding of the U.S. deficit. The TIC and other official measures of inflow and outflow provide an indication of the demand by foreign central banks for U.S. government debt.

European economic indicators

The European Union includes 15 member nations. The currency used in all but three of these nations is the euro. The 12 nations that share the euro are collectively known as the Economic and Monetary Union

(EMU). The European Central Bank (ECB) dictates the monetary policy of the EMU, which is the second largest economic power in the world, second only to the United States. The 2009 GDP of the EMU was an estimated $14.51 trillion U.S. dollars. The EMU has highly developed fixed income, equity, and futures markets and is the second most attractive market for both domestic and international investments. In the past, the European Union has failed to attract foreign direct investment or large capital flows. It has been responsible for about 45 percent of the total world capital outflow and only about 19 percent of capital inflows because of the ability of the United States to maintain solid returns on its assets. Recently, the euro has become a more established currency with more nations willing to hold euros in reserve. Capital inflows have increased and demand for the euro has increased.

The EMU is both a trade- and capital-flow driven economy that is also service-oriented with no trade deficit or surplus. Exports by the EMU account for 16 percent of world trade exports, while imports account for 18.3 percent of total world imports. The magnitude of the EMU's trade with other nations makes it a significant power in international trade. The EMU provides for its individual member nations to unite and negotiate under one monetary system, particularly against the United States, which is its largest trading partner. Leading export markets are the United States, Russia, Switzerland, Turkey, China, Japan, and Poland. Leading import markets are China, the United States, Russia, Norway, Switzerland, and Japan.

Service-oriented sectors of the economy accounted for 70.5 percent of the EMU's GDP in 2006. Mining, utilities, and manufacturing accounted for only 27.3 percent of the GDP because many companies that produce finished goods outsource manufacturing activities to Asia while concentrating domestically on research, innovation, design, and marketing.

The EU's expansion in international trade has been responsible for bringing about growth in the euro as a reserve currency. Foreign nations must maintain large reserves of the currencies of major trading partners to reduce transaction costs and the risk inherent in currency exchanges. Before the establishment of the EU and the euro, other nations found it impractical to hold large reserves of each individual European currency. Instead, currency reserves were held in U.S. dollars, and most international trades involved the U.S. dollar, British pound, and the Japanese yen. Since the establishment of the EU, many foreign reserve assets have begun to shift in favor of the euro, and this shift is expected to continue as the EU expands its position as one of the major trading partners for nations around the globe.

The ECB uses four main categories of open market operations to influence interest rates, manage liquidity, and signal monetary stance: main refinancing operations, longer-term refinancing options, fine-tuned operations, and structural operations. The ECB's main refinancing operations provide regular liquidity through reverse transactions conducted on a weekly basis with a maturity of two weeks. A reverse transaction involves buying or selling assets under a repurchase agreement — an agreement to buy the assets back within a certain time period. This type of open market operation provides refinancing to the financial sector. Longer-term financing operations provide liquidity through reverse transactions conducted on a monthly basis with a maturity of three months. This type of operation provides counterparties with additional longer-term financing. Fine tuning operations are executed in response to particular situations. The purpose is to manage liquidity in the market and influence interest rates, particularly in an effort to smooth the effects that unexpected liquidity fluctuations have on interest rates. Structural operations involve the issuance of reverse transactions, debt certificates, and outright transactions, when the ECB feels the need to adjust the structural position of the euro system via the financial sector. Structural operations may be carried out on a regular or irregular basis.

The ECB provides a minimum bid rate, which is the level of borrowing that the ECB offers to member nations' central banks. This rate is subject to change as a result of policy decision making at bi-weekly ECB meetings. Inflation is of great concern to the ECB, which will intervene in foreign exchange markets if it believes inflation is imminent. The ECB may keep interest rates at high levels to prevent inflation. The ECB does not target specific exchange rates but recognizes exchange rates will affect price stability. The ECB factors exchange rates into its policy decisions. Any comments made by the members of the ECB's Governing Council are of concern to market participants because such comments frequently move the euro. The ECB publishes a monthly bulletin detailing changes in its perception of economic conditions and its analysis of economic developments. Traders monitor this bulletin for indications of changes in the bias of monetary policy.

Traders in the euro must analyze the economic and political developments in GDP, inflation, and unemployment for all member countries of the EMU. Because France, Germany, and Italy are the largest nations in the EMU, the individual economic data must be analyzed alongside the economic data of the overall EMU.

TIP: Economic indicators for the euro must be analyzed together with indicators of the non-euro member nations of the EU.

Eleven members of the European Union — Bulgaria, the Czech Republic, Denmark, Estonia, Hungary, Latvia, Lithuania, Poland, Romania, Sweden, and the United Kingdom — have not introduced the euro, but their economies are closely linked to the euro. It is important to be aware of how the economic indicators of these countries affect the value of the euro.

European Gross Domestic Product (GDP)

To produce a satisfactory estimate, a preliminary GDP is issued after data is collected from a sufficient number of European countries. This data is usually collected from France, Germany, and the Netherlands. Italy is not included in preliminary GDP data but is added in a final computation of the GDP. The yearly GDPs for the 15 nations of the EU and the 12 nations of the EMU are computed simply as the sum of the individual GDPs. However, quarterly estimates require more complex calculations to account for the three nations, Greece, Ireland, and Luxemburg, which do not produce quarterly account data. Portugal produces only partial quarterly account data, which lags in time. As a result, the quarterly computation of GDP for the EU nations and EMU nations is based on data collected from a group of nations that accounts for more than 95 percent of the total GDP of the EU.

Harmonized Index of Consumer Prices (HICP)

The EU HICP is published on a monthly basis. Laws provide that the HICP be designed for international comparisons. A specific index — the Monetary Union Index of Consumer Prices (MUIP) — is published for the 11 founding EMU member nations that use the euro. Price data is compiled from each government's statistical agency. Each nation is required to provide 100 indexes to be used in the computation of HICP. The national HICPs are totaled as weighted averages with weights specific to each nation. The HICP is released at the end of the month, following a reference period of about ten days after the publication of national consumer price indexes from France and Spain, the final countries of the EMU to release their CPIs. The HICP release serves as the reference inflation index for the ECB, which strives to keep consumer price inflation in the range of 0 percent to 2 percent.

M3

A broader measure of European money supply is established by the M3, a measure of the amount of money that is commercially available within an economic system, including notes, coins, and bank deposits. The ECB considers the M3 as a key measure of inflation. The first reference value ever established for M3 was set at 4.5 percent growth in 1998. This reference value provides for inflation below 2 percent, trend growth in the range of 2 percent to 2.5 percent, and long-term decline in the range of 0.5 percent to 1 percent. Growth rate is measured as a three-month moving average to prevent monthly volatility from distorting data from the aggregates. The ECB does not impose limits on M3 growth; therefore, there is no automatic procedure put into place when M3 growth diverges from the reference value. The ECB considers the M3 to be a key indicator of growth, but it also accounts for changes in other monetary aggregates.

Industrial production (IP)

Industrial production (IP) data encompasses four major subcategories of production that are seasonally adjusted — manufacturing, mining, construction, and energy. The manufacturing component includes four main product groups — capital goods, basic and producer goods, consumer durables, and consumer non-durables. The market tends to focus on annual rates of change and monthly-adjusted IP estimates.

Although the market reacts to French IP figures, Germany's IP is the most important for currency traders, because it is the largest country among the euro nations. Initial IP figures are released but are subject to revision, based on a subset of the data to be used in the final release. The final release is published when the full dataset becomes available. The initial release may also include indicators from the Finance Ministry of the expected direction of the revised data.

Unemployment

Unemployment data is released monthly in Germany, the largest economy in Europe, by the Federal Labor Office (FLO), along with changes from the previous month in both seasonally adjusted (SA) and non-seasonally adjusted (NSA) data. Non-seasonally adjusted unemployment data includes vacancies, the number of employed, and the number of short-shift working arrangements. Within hours of the FLO release, the Bundesbank release of seasonally adjusted unemployment data occurs.

Currency traders must interpret news reports carefully, so decisions are not made based on rumors and incorrect data. Weeks before the release of unemployment data, rumors spread about expected results. These rumors are usually based on imprecise data, and the international press sometimes misinterprets comments from German officials. On the day preceding the official releases of data, a trade union source typically leaks the official non-seasonally adjusted data in millions of dollars. When data is reported by Reuters, as provided by "sources for the NSA level of unemployment," the data is official.

IFO survey

As the largest economy in Europe, Germany is responsible for more than 20 percent of the total European GDP. Any insight into German business and economic conditions is considered an insight into the whole of Europe. The IFO survey, conducted by the Institut für Wirtschaftsforschung an der Universität München, provides data compiled from more than 7,000 German businesses. The survey requests that these businesses provide an assessment of the German business climate and short-term plans. An initial publication of survey results includes the business climate headline figure and two equally weighted sub indexes — current business expectations and business conditions. A typical range of indices is 80 to 120, with the high value indicating greater business confidence. Measured values are most valuable when measured against previously compiled data.

Budget deficits

Individual European nations are governed by the Stability and Growth Pact, which dictates that deficits must be kept below 3 percent of the GDP. Individual countries set target rates to reduce deficits further. Market participants closely watch failure of these countries to meet their target rates because this can affect the value of the euro.

British economic indicators

The United Kingdom is the sixth largest economy in the world, with a GDP estimate in 2009 of $2.19 trillion U.S. dollars. The United Kingdom has benefited from a history of strong growth, expanding output, low unemployment, and strong consumer consumption. The nation's strength in the housing market is partly responsible for its strength in consumer consumption. The service-oriented economy includes a manufacturing sector that continues to represent smaller portions of the GDP and accounts for about one-fifth of the nation's output. The capital market systems are the most advanced financial systems in the world with banking and finance accounting for the largest percentage of the GDP. Though the GDP is primarily based on services, the United Kingdom is also one of the world's largest producers and exporters of natural gas to the EU. The energy production industry accounts for 5.1 percent of the GDP. The increasing demand for energy and rising energy costs continues to benefit the large number of U.K. oil exporters.

The primary U.K. import is finished goods, and the United Kingdom maintains a consistent trade deficit. Its largest overall trading partner, the EU, accounts for more than 52 percent of all import and export activities. On an individual basis, however, the United Kingdom's largest trading partner is the United States, followed by China, Switzerland, and Russia.

Why the UK does not want to adopt the Euro

The United Kingdom has rejected an adoption of the euro as its currency because the government is satisfied that its sound macroeconomic policies have worked well for the country. The United Kingdom rejects the idea of having to adjust its interest rates to reflect equivalent rates of euro nations. The United Kingdom's existing fiscal and monetary policies have outperformed those of most major economies through recent economic downturns, including that of the EU. The United Kingdom treasury specifies five economic conditions that must be met before the United Kingdom will consider adopting the euro. First, there must be a sustainable convergence of economic structures and business cycles between the United Kingdom and EMU member nations, so U.K. citizens are able to live comfortably with euro interest rates on a permanent basis. Second, there must be enough flexibility to sustain economic change. Third, joining the EMU must create an environment that encourages firms to invest in the United Kingdom. Fourth, joining the EMU must have a positive impact on the competitiveness of the U.K. financial services industry. Finally, joining the EMU must promote growth and stability in employment.

The political structure of the United Kingdom is set up so government officials are very concerned about voter approval. If voters do not support a conversion to euro, it is not likely that membership in the EMU will occur.

Arguments for a conversion to euro include:
- A single currency would promote price transparency.
- The euro is the second most important reserve currency after the U.S. dollar.
- There would be efficiency in the allocation of capital in Europe through integration of national financial markets of the EU.
- Sustained low inflation under the guidance of the ECB would reduce long-term interest rates and stimulate sustained economic growth.
- There would be uncertainty in exchange rates for U.K. businesses and lower transaction costs and risks.
- U.K. membership with the EMU would increase the political clout of the EMU.

Arguments against a conversion to euro include:
- Historically, currency unions have collapsed.
- EMU criteria, as outlined by the Stability and Growth Pact, are too strict.
- A conversion would require a permanent transfer of existing domestic monetary authority to the ECB.
- Adjusting to the new currency would require large transaction costs.
- The people are anxious about which country would dominate the ECB.
- The lack of monetary flexibility would require that the United Kingdom have more flexibility in housing and labor markets.
- The political and economic instabilities of one nation could affect the euro and negatively affect exchange rates for countries with otherwise healthy economies.

The goal of the U.K. open market operations is to implement changes in the bank repo rate while assuring continued stability in the banking system and adequate liquidity in the market. The bank repo rate is the rate used in U.K. monetary policy to meet targets for inflation set by the Treasury. This rate is applied to the BOE's own market operations, such as short-term lending. Changes to the bank repo rate affect commercial bank rates for borrowing and saving. Any attempt to increase the repo rate represents an attempt to cut inflation, and any attempt to decrease rates indicates that the government wants to stimulate expansion and growth.

The goals of U.K. open market operations correlate with the objectives of the BOE, whose three primary objectives are to maintain integrity and value in the currency, maintain stability in the financial system, and ensure the effectiveness of the financial services industry. To ensure liquidity, the BOE conducts daily open market operations to sell or buy short-term fixed income instruments of the government. If this is not sufficient to achieve necessary liquidity, the BOE conducts additional overnight operations.

The United Kingdom is a service-oriented economy with indicators that describe service and non-service sectors of the economy.

Industrial Production (IP) index

The IP index measures the change in output from the manufacturing, quarry, and mining industries as well as output from electric, gas, and water suppliers. Output is defined as the physical quantity of items produced. It differs from sales volume, which measures quantity and price. The U.K. IP index includes the production of goods and power for domestic sales and for export. IP accounts for about 23 percent of the U.K.'s GDP and provides an indication of the current state of the economy.

Employment

The U.K. Office of National Statistics conducts a monthly survey, which divides the working age population into three classifications and provides explanatory and descriptive information on each category. These classifications include "employed," "unemployed," and "not in the labor force." The resulting data provide information on major labor market trends, such as unemployment, hours worked, labor force participation, and shifts in employment. The timely, monthly distribution of the compiled data provides market participants with a good measure of the strength of the U.K. economy.

Retail Price Index (RPI)

The RPI is a measure of the change in price of a basket of consumer goods. Although market participants are interested in the RPI, they are more concerned with the measure when it excludes mortgagee interest payments. The RPI, exclusive of mortgage interest payments, is called the RPI-X. The RPI-X is used by the Treasury to set inflation targets for the BOE. The current inflation target is set to 2 percent of the annual growth in RPI-X.

Housing starts

Housing starts are a monthly measure of the number of residential building construction starts in a given month. The housing market is the industry primarily responsible for sustaining the nation's economic performance.

Purchasing Manager's Index (PMI)

The PMI is a weighted average of seasonally adjusted measures of output, inventory, new orders, and employment. Data is compiled from a monthly survey conducted by the Chartered Institute of Purchasing and Supply. Index values below 50 percent indicate a contracting economy and values above 50 indicate an expanding economy.

Switzerland economic indicators

Switzerland is the 38th largest economy in the world, with an estimated 2009 GDP of more than $317 billion. Though relatively small, Switzerland has one of the wealthiest per capita economies in the world. Its technological advances and prosperity contribute to an economic stability that rivals that of larger economies. Switzerland enjoys prosperity as the result of technical expertise in banking, manufacturing, and tourism; advances in chemical and pharmaceuticals; and precision in instrumentation, machinery, and watches.

Switzerland's financial system is also known for historically protecting the identity of its investors. These aspects of the Swiss infrastructure, combined with a lengthy history of political stability, have given Switzerland a reputation as a financial safe haven. Switzerland is the world's largest destination for offshore capital. The nation is credited with attracting more than 35 percent of the world's private wealth management business, and holds in excess of $2 trillion in offshore assets, complemented by a large and highly advanced insurance and banking system that makes up about 70 percent of the Switzerland GDP.

Consequently, the insurance and banking systems employ more than 50 percent of the population. During times of international risk aversion, capital flows tend to drive the economy, while trade flows drive the economy during times of risk seeking. Trade flows are an important aspect of the economy and about two-thirds of all trade is with Europe. Switzerland's leading export markets are Germany, the United States, Italy, France, and the United Kingdom. Its leading import markets are Germany, Italy, France, the United States, and the Netherlands.

Historically, trade flows of merchandise have caused fluctuations in the economy from deficits to surplus. In recent years, the economy has sustained a surplus. In fact, the surplus reached a high of 24.26 percent of the GDP in 2006 (15.38 percent in 2008). With the exception of Norway, this figure represents the highest surplus experienced by any industrialized nation. The surplus is directly related to the large amount of foreign direct investment. Despite the low yields offered by Switzerland, the safety of capital and privacy in investments lures many foreign investors to invest in the nation.

The Swiss National Bank (SNB) uses Target Interest Rate Range and open market operations to implement monetary policy. Target Interest Rate Range is the target range for its three-month interest rate, known as the Swiss LIBOR rate. The Swiss LIBOR rate is the most important money market rate for Swiss franc investments and is chosen as the target rate. Any change to the rate is documented with an explanation of the change as it relates to the economy of the country. The range typically has a 100 basis-point spread that is revised at least once per quarter.

Open market operations include what is known as repo transactions. A repo transaction involves a borrower and a lender. The borrower sells securities to the lender with an agreement to repurchase securities of the same quantity and type at a later date. Repo transactions are similar to secured loans offered by banking institutions in the United States, where the borrower pays the lender interest on the cash secured by the account. Repo transactions generally have short periods of maturity, usually in the range of one day to a few weeks. The SNB uses these transactions to manipulate undesirable movement in the three-month LIBOR rate. To prevent increases in the LIBOR rate from rising above the SNB target rate, the SNB may use repo transactions to provide commercial banks with additional liquidity. Repo transactions are carried out with lowered repo rates to create the necessary liquidity. The SNB may increase repo transaction rates to reduce liquidity or create an increase in the three-month LIBOR rate.

The SNB provides market participants with its assessment of the current domestic situation through its publications. The SNB publishes a review of monetary policies and a detailed assessment of the current state of the economy in its quarterly bulletin. The SNB also publishes a monthly bulletin that provides a short review of economic developments.

Switzerland Gross Domestic Product (GDP)

The GDP, the measure of total production and consumption of Switzerland's goods and services, includes household, government, and business expenditures as well as the net foreign purchases. A GDP price deflator is used to convert current price output into constant dollar GDP. The data is then used to determine where Switzerland falls in the business cycle. Fast growth indicates inflation and low or no growth indicates a recessionary or weak economy.

Consumer Price Index (CPI)

The CPI is calculated on a monthly basis and is the key measure of inflation. It considers all retail prices paid in Switzerland for a basket of goods. The Swiss computation falls in line with international practice, which dictates that the commodities in the CPI include the goods and services that are part of the private consumption aggregate according to Swiss national accounts. The basket of goods does not include transfer expenditures, such as social insurance, direct taxation, and health insurance premiums.

Production Index

The production index is a measure of change in the volume of industrial production or physical output from producers. This index is released quarterly.

Retail sales

Retail sales data is published 40 days following the month referred to in the retail sales report. The data is used as an indicator of consumer spending, which is not seasonally adjusted.

Balance of payments

Balance of payments is used to describe account transactions collectively with the rest of the international community. The current account balance includes the balance of trade plus service portion. The balance of payments indicates the current account balance, which has always been strong. Any change, either positive or negative, is expected to generate substantial flows in the market.

Konjunkturforschungsstelle der ETH, Zurich (KoF) leading indicators

The Swiss Institute for Business Cycle Research publishes a report of the leading KoF indicators, generally used to assess the future health of the Swiss economy. The report contains six components — the change in manufacturers' orders and manufacturers' order backlog; manufacturers' expected purchase plans for the next three months; construction order backlogs; judgment of stocks in the wholesale business; and consumer perception of consumers' financial conditions.

Japanese economic indicators

Japan is the third-largest economy in the world, with a GDP estimate of $4.1 trillion in 2009. Japan has a manufacturing-oriented economy that accounts for about 20 percent of the GDP. Japan exports more than $500 billion in goods per year. Despite its structural deficiencies, Japan maintains a consistent trade surplus, which creates a demand for the yen. Japan also imports large amounts of raw materials for the production of goods. The United States and China are its biggest import and export markets. China, being an inexpensive-goods-producing nation, surpassed the United States in 2003 to become Japan's largest source of imports. Leading export markets are the United States, China, South Korea, Taiwan, and Hong Kong. Leading import markets are China, the United States, Saudi Arabia, Australia, the United Arab Emirates, and Indonesia.

Japan's open-market operations are focused on controlling the overnight call rate. The BOJ has maintained a zero interest rate policy for years. As a result, the Japanese cannot lower rates to stimulate growth, liquidity, or consumption. The only method of manipulating liquidity is through their open market operations. They buy and sell repos, bills, and government bonds, with a zero interest target on the overnight call rate.

The BOJ has considered implementing methods to address its nonperforming loans such as inflation targeting, repacking bad debts and selling them at a discount, and nationalizing some private banks. However, no policy has been decided on or implemented.

Gross Domestic Product

Japan's GDP, a broad measure of total production and consumption of goods and services, is measured and released quarterly and annually. The measure includes total household, business, and government expenditures as well as the net foreign purchases. A GDP price deflator is used to convert current price output into constant dollar GDP. Preliminary reports of the data have been most significant to market participants.

Industrial Production (IP) index

The industrial production index measures the strength of the manufacturing, mining, and utility industries. The index includes the production of goods for domestic sales and export, and excludes production in the construction, agriculture, transportation, finance, trades, communication, and service industries. It also excludes government output and imports. Each component of the measure is weighted according to its importance during the base period. Market participants examine the correlation of IP and inventory accumulation with total output to gain insight into the current state of the economy.

Employment

The Management and Coordination Agency of Japan compiles and releases employment figures on a monthly basis. Data is obtained from a survey of the current labor force. The release provides an indication of Japan's overall unemployment and the number of available jobs. The timeliness of this release makes it one of the top indicators of economic activity.

Balance of payments

Balance of payment data includes information on capital flows, goods, services, and investment income. Data is compiled and released on both a monthly and semiannual basis. The figures provide currency market participants with an indication of international transactions and provide the BOJ with a gauge of international trade.

Tankan survey

The Tankan survey is a short-term economic survey of Japanese business enterprises. The survey is published quarterly to document results from more than 9,000 small, medium, large, and principal Japanese enterprises. This provides an overall indication of the Japanese business climate.

Australian economic indicators

Australia has the fifth-largest GDP in the Asian-Pacific region, 18th in the world, with a 2009 estimate of more than $824 billion. The relatively small economy has a per capita GDP comparable to many Western European nations. Australia's economy is service-oriented with about 79 percent of the GDP attributable to finance, property, and business-service industries. Manufacturing dominates export activities, with rural and mineral exports accounting for more than 60 percent of all manufacturing exports. The economy is sensitive to commodity price changes, and the country maintains a trade deficit. The largest export markets are Japan, China, South Korea, India, the United States, New Zealand, and the United Kingdom. The largest import markets are China, the United States, Japan, Singapore, Germany, Thailand, the United Kingdom, and Malaysia.

Leading exports are to Japan and the Association of Southeast Asian Nations (ASEAN). The ASEAN includes Brunei, Cambodia, Indonesia,

Laos, Malaysia, Myanmar, the Philippines, Singapore, Thailand, and Vietnam. As a result, the Australian economy appears to be sensitive to the state of the nations of the ASEAN. However, history has shown that the Australian economy is not only able to withstand an Asian crisis but is also able to grow during such a crisis. Australia's sound foundation and strong domestic consumption provide stability for the nation. Consumption has steadily risen since the 1980s. Consumer consumption, rather than exports, is the more important indicator to watch during global economic slowdown.

The Reserve Bank of Australia (RBA) establishes the cash rate as the target rate for open market operations. The cash rate is the overnight rate charged for loans between financial entities. The cash rate should have some correlation with money market interest rates. Changes in monetary policy have a direct impact on the interest-rate structure used in the financial system as well as the movement of currency. Daily open-market operations focus on managing money-market liquidity provided to commercial banks by keeping the cash rate close to the established target rate. To increase the cash rate, the RBA decreases the supply of short-dated repurchase agreements at a lower interest rate than the existing cash rate.

Australia has maintained a floating exchange rate since the early 1980s. The RBA engages in foreign exchange market operations when the market threatens to be excessively volatile or the exchange rate moves opposite to the way it should move based on underlying economic fundamentals. The RBA uses a trade-weighted index and its cross rate with the U.S. dollar to determine whether to intervene to attempt to stabilize market conditions rather than meet exchange rate targets.

Gross Domestic Product (GDP)

The GDP measures the total production of goods and services in Australia. It includes total household, business, and government expenditures as well as net foreign purchases. A GDP price deflator is used to convert current price output into constant dollar GDP. Fast growth is perceived by market participants as inflationary, and slow growth is perceived as recessionary or a weakened economy.

Producer Price Index (PPI)

The PPI is a group of individual indexes that measure the average change in selling prices that producers receive for their output. The Australian PPI is released quarterly. The PPI accounts for changes in just about every goods-producing industry including manufacturing, agriculture, forestry, electric utilities, natural gas, mining, and fisheries. Foreign exchange markets tend to focus on the PPI of seasonally adjusted finished goods and monthly, quarterly, semi-annual, and annual changes.

Consumer Price Index (CPI)

The CPI measures quarterly changes in price of a basket of goods and services. It considers a high proportion of expenditures by metropolitan households and includes food, health, housing, transportation, and education. Monetary policy changes affect this index, which is the indicator of inflation.

Balance of goods and services

The balance of goods and services is a measure of international trade in goods and services, assessed based on the balance of payments. This measure is acquired from an assessment of general merchandise exports and imports as reported by international trade statistics compiled from Australian Customs Service records. The information is released monthly.

Private consumption

Private consumption is a measure of national accounts, which indicates the current expenditure by households and producers of private nonprofit services to households. Private consumption includes the purchase of both durable and non-durable goods. It excludes expenditures for real estate and capital expenditures by unincorporated business enterprises. This measure indicates private consumption, which is a measure of resilience in the Australian economy.

New Zealand economic indicators

New Zealand has a small economy, with a GDP estimate in 2009 of more than $114.9 billion, 61st in the world. The population of New Zealand is about half that of the city of New York. The nation is shifting from a historically agricultural economy to a more knowledge-based economy with skilled employment and high value-added production. New Zealand has highly developed manufacturing and servicing sectors, but the agricultural sector is responsible for producing most of the nation's exports. The New Zealand economy is trade-oriented, with exports of goods and services accounting for about one-fourth of the GDP. The leading markets for both import and export include Australia, the United States, Japan, and China. Together, Australia and Japan account for 31.6 percent of New Zealand's trade activity. The small economy and the reliance on trade make New Zealand sensitive to global trading performance, especially the performance of its major trading partners. New Zealand rarely releases economic indicators, but the following are of importance.

Gross Domestic Product

The GDP measures the total production and consumption of goods and services in New Zealand. It includes total household, business, and government expenditures, as well as the net foreign purchases. A GDP price deflator is used to convert current price output into constant dollar GDP. Market participants perceive fast growth as inflationary and slow growth as a weakened economy.

Consumer Price Index

The CPI measures quarterly changes in price of a basket of goods and services. It considers a high proportion of expenditures by metropolitan households and includes food, health, housing, transportation, and education. Monetary policy changes affect this index, which is the indicator of inflation.

Balance of goods and services

Balance of payments statements record the value of New Zealand transactions for goods, services, income, and transfers with the rest of the international community. The statements also record changes in New Zealand's financial claims on the international community and liabilities to the international community. New Zealand also publishes an International Position statement, which shows the stocks of the nation's international financial assets and liabilities at specific times.

Private consumption

Private consumption is a measure of national accounts and indicates the current expenditure by households and producers of private nonprofit services to households. Private consumption includes the purchase of both durable and non-durable goods. It excludes expenditures for real estate and capital expenditures by unincorporated business enterprises.

Producer Price Index

The New Zealand PPI is released quarterly. It accounts for changes in just about every goods-producing industry, including manufacturing, agriculture, forestry, electric utilities, natural gas, mining, and fisheries.

Foreign exchange markets tend to focus on the PPI of seasonally adjusted finished goods and monthly, quarterly, semi-annual, and annual changes.

Canadian economic indicators

Canada represents the 11th-largest economy in the world, with a GDP estimate in 2009 of more than $1.285 trillion. Canada has experienced consistent growth since 1991. Traditionally, the economy was based on the exploitation and export of natural resources. Canada exported 55.73 billion kWh of electricity in 2008. The nation has grown to become the seventh-largest producer of gold, and the seventh-largest producer and fifth-largest exporter of oil. Even so, nearly two-thirds of the GDP is derived from the service sector, which employs three quarters of the population. The strength of the service sector is partly due to a trend in subcontracting business services. Manufacturing and resources account for more than 25 percent of the nation's exports and provide the primary source of income for a number of Canadian provinces. Canada exports more than 73 percent of its goods to the United States, which makes Canada sensitive to the health of the U.S. economy. The leading export markets are the United States, the United Kingdom, and Japan. The leading import markets are the United States, China, and Mexico.

The Canadian Large Value Transfer System (LVTS) provides the Bank of Canada (BOC) with the framework to implement monetary policy. The LVTS is an electronic platform that allows commercial banks to borrow and lend overnight money to each other so that they may fund their daily transactions. The interest applied to these overnight transactions by the BOC is called the overnight rate or bank rate. This rate is used to control inflation. Changes in the bank rate affect all other interest rates, inclusive of mortgage interest rates and the prime rate charged by commercial banks. The BOC sometimes manipulates bank rates higher or lower than the current market interest rates when the overnight lending rate trades above or below the target. The BOC releases publications that provide indications of the state of the economy at regular intervals. These publications include the *Monetary Policy Report* and the *Bank of Canada Review*. The *Monetary Policy Report* evaluates the current economic environment and provides implications for inflation. The *Bank of Canada Review* offers quarterly feature articles, speeches, commentary, and important announcements.

Gross Domestic Product

The GDP is the yearly total value of all goods and services produced within Canada. It is a measure of income generated by production, often referred to as economic output. Canada's GDP includes only final goods and services and excludes those goods and services used to produce an end product. This method of accounting for goods and services prevents any output from being counted more than once.

Producer Price Index (PPI)

The Canadian PPI accounts for changes for just about every goods-producing industry, including manufacturing, agriculture, forestry, electric utilities, natural gas, mining, and fisheries. Foreign exchange markets tend to focus on the PPI of seasonally adjusted finished goods and monthly, quarterly, semi-annual, and annual changes.

Consumer Price Index (CPI)

The CPI measures the average rate of increase in consumer prices. Usually when inflation is indicated, it presumes that general price increases have caused a decline in the currency's purchasing power. It is usually presented as the percentage increase in the CPI. In Canada, the federal government and BOC establish inflation policy that attempts to keep inflation within a target range of 1 percent to 3 percent.

Unemployment

The unemployment rate is released as the number of persons employed as a percentage of the labor force.

Balance of trade

The balance of trade indicates the nation's trade in goods and services. The balance of trade measures the difference between the value of goods and services exported and those imported. Trades for products, such as raw materials, agricultural goods, and manufactured goods as well as transportation and travel associated with such trades are included in the figure. If exports exceed imports, a trade surplus or positive trade balance is indicated. If, on the other hand, imports exceed exports, a trade deficit or negative balance of trade is indicated.

Consumer consumption

Consumer buying is a measure of national accounts, indicating the current expenditure by households and producers of private nonprofit services to households. Consumer buying includes the purchase of both durable and non-durable goods. It excludes expenditures for real estate and capital expenditures by unincorporated business enterprises.

Chapter 6

Technical Analysis

ending reports, statistical releases, revisions to economic indicators, and other releases of fundamental data often cause violent market reactions in one direction or the other, but it is difficult to convert that qualitative information into specific price predictions. Fundamental analysis provides long-term forecasts of exchange rate movements, but technical analysis is the most successful and widely used method for analyzing the forex market and for deciding exactly when to buy and sell. Technical analysis ignores the fundamental factors and concentrates on price action in the currency market, studying historical price movements, and developing mathematical models or pattern recognition, in order to predict future prices. Currency traders use these models and patterns to take position in the currency market.

Technical traders believe currency prices in the forex market follow established patterns, determined primarily by efficiency in the market, quick trading times — often less than one minute — and the growing number of participating traders. Technical analysis is primarily used to analyze and trade short-term price movements, establish stop-loss safeguards, and set profit targets.

The multitude of factors used in fundamental analysis can lead to an information overload. Some traders resort to methods of technical analysis because they feel unable to sort through the vast amount of information associated with a trade. Technical analysis is thought to transform all the fundamental factors that influence the market into a simple analytical tool, called prices. Some technical strategies assume that economic fundamentals are automatically reflected in a currency's price movements and there is no need to consider them any further. However, traders who opt for technical analysis cannot completely ignore the fundamentals of trading. A currency trader who does not understand the particulars of a market and the underlying elements behind price movements is relying on guesswork.

Technical analysis considers four price fields that are available to traders at any given time:

- **Open**: The price at which a currency sells at the beginning of a time interval

- **Close**: The price at which a currency sells at the end of the same time interval

- **High**: The highest price at which a currency sells during the time interval

- **Low**: The lowest price at which a currency sells during a time interval

Most technical evaluations include charts of price changes over periods of time that emphasize selected characteristics of price motion. Technical evaluations attempts to predict market direction or generate buy and sell indicators based on patterns in price movement.

One of the advantages of technical analysis is it provides a visual picture of data. Technical analysis assumes historical patterns repeat themselves and rejects the belief that market price fluctuations are unpredictable or random. Analysis suggests that when a trend moves in one particular direction, it has a tendency to continue in that direction for some time interval — minutes, days, or pips. This time interval is identified and used for charting and analyzing market data.

TIP: Trading decisions should never be made based on technical indicators alone.

The best technical strategies combine a comparison of charts with evaluation of several economic indicators. The economic indicators confirm that certain patterns in price movement are occurring in response to the same types of economic conditions that have caused them in the past. Historical patterns can be expected to repeat themselves. If the economic indicators show that price movements are caused by some unprecedented event, such as a natural disaster or political unrest, the outcome cannot be predicted with any degree of certainty.

Charts and Trends

Technical traders typically use charts displaying market data to determine market trends combined with important technical indicators, such as points of support and resistance. The proper identification of ongoing trends and recurring patterns that disrupt the continuity of trend lines is important to currency traders. The patterns displayed by charted data can be divided into two categories — reversal patterns and continuation patterns. Reversal patterns indicate that a price that has been moving in one direction is about to start moving in the opposite direction; a market entry point is being reached (time to buy); or it may be time to liquidate (sell) an open position. Continuation patterns occur when a trend movement is interrupted for a time and then continues in the direction of the original trend. *See the following section "Types of Charts" for examples of how patterns of market data are displayed on charts.*

Currency price movements are driven by two factors: large interbank trades and the psychology of currency speculators. When speculators believe prices will rise, they enter the market and push prices up. When they expect prices to fall, they exit the market, causing prices to drop. The ups and downs of a price chart present a visual picture of market sentiment.

Trends

Market trend shows the general direction of the market's broad movement. Trend lines are determined by connecting two points on a linear graph of historical data describing a particular market. The two points may be either peaks or troughs in the data. Even when the data appears to fluctuate in a series of ups and downs, a trend line or multiple trend lines can be determined. Although two points are often sufficient to establish a trend line, a connection of several peaks or troughs provides a more vivid picture of true market trend. Trends may be established for any chosen time period, over a period of minutes, days, or months. They do not necessarily have to represent an upward or downward pattern. Market data may settle into consolidated patterns that do not point firmly in either direction. Some of the more familiar charting patterns are discussed below.

A common trading technique involves analyzing the intersection of trend lines with the most recent prices. A downward trend intersecting with the most recent prices indicates that a trader should buy. An upward trend line intersecting with the most recent prices indicates that the trader should sell.

Trend lines

Trends are defined by price actions. On a graph showing fluctuations in a currency's price, an uptrend represents progressively higher lows, and a downtrend represents progressively lower highs. An uptrend implies that prices will continue to rise for some time period, and a downtrend implies that prices will continue to fall. Trend lines are the simplest tools for determining the direction of a trend. The theory is that in an uptrend, traders should draw a straight line connecting the lowest low point to the highest high point; in a downtrend, the line should be drawn from the highest low point to the lowest high point. Prices are expected to fall within these boundaries. The difficulty is deciding where to draw such lines. Should the lines be drawn using closing price highs and lows or the highs and lows of a particular time period? Further, should the lines be adjusted to account for spikes in the data, or should spikes in the data be ignored? Finally, should trend lines be adjusted based on the chosen scale of the chart? All of these questions must be considered when creating trend lines.

How is a currency's closing price determined?

The foreign exchange market opens at 5 p.m. EST on Sunday and closes at 4 p.m. EST on Friday. During this period, the market is running 24 hours a day because there is always a trading exchange open somewhere in the world. Between the Friday close and the Sunday open, the forex market does not trade. Technically, the opening prices for the week are the initial trading prices on Sunday, and the closing prices for the week are those of the last trade on Friday.

In the news, you will often hear quotes for the opening and closing prices for currency pairs on a particular day. These quotes are the closing prices for an individual market, usually in the country or region where that news source is based. There are several forex markets within each of three main regions — North America, Asia, and Europe — each with its own open and close times. The main North America market is in New York; in Asia it is in Tokyo; and in Europe, it is in London. In North American media, the closing price typically refers to the closing price of the New York forex market.

Channel trading strategy

Advocates of trend lines agree — trend lines should be used to capture the natural rhythms of buying and selling data. As a result, a more sophisticated use of trend lines involves designing trend line channels. These channels are determined by drawing a line connecting the lows of price actions (the bottom of the channel) and another line connecting the highs of price action (the top of the channel). The trading strategy is to purchase when the price is at, or near, the support trend line (the bottom line of the channel), and sell when it approaches the line of resistance (the upper line of the channel). The objective is to buy cheap and sell at profit several times over the length of a price action.

This strategy is very profitable, as long as the price remains within the chosen channel. When the price breaks out of the channel, the currency trader must consider several factors and establish parameters for his or her measurement. The trader must decide what constitutes a break of a trend line. Piercing the line just once could constitute a break, or the trader might decide that a break does not occur until the price goes past the trend line and stays there. If the price is required to extend beyond the line, the trader must determine by how much the price has to extend to constitute a break. Most importantly, the trader must determine whether a single break of the trend line, for a single price point, is sufficient to be considered a true break. There is no absolute answer, but some rules can be applied with a degree of assurance.

A break in a trend line is not expected to predict a definite change of trend, though there are situations in which a break signifies the reversal of price action. A break in a trend line simply signifies that a trend might be ending. What typically follows a break in trend is not a reversal of the trend but consolidation, a period during which the price fluctuates up and down within the boundaries of a channel. This can be confusing, because price actions may generate many false breakouts while still continuing to follow the trend.

A simple piercing of a trend line during a single period is not usually considered a true break. A close above or below the trend line is more characteristic of a break. For example, in the case of a downtrend line, such a close would indicate that buyers have overwhelmed sellers who were initially beating them out. A trend line break requires a closing price beyond the trend line. Closing prices are analyzed because the premise of technical analysis is that though the past price action is significant, the more recent past is most important. If the price over the next few periods stays beyond the trend line, the trend may be changing. If the price returns to the trend line but then breaks off again, a change might or might not have occurred.

Types of charts

Most forex trading platforms offer a charting package that consists of a selection of price charts with various features that you can customize to fit your trading strategy. The same live data is presented in several types of charts. The most commonly used types are described below.

TIP: A picture is worth a thousand words: pricing charts online.

Go online and experience live pricing charts for yourself. Most of them have a menu bar across the top of the chart that lets you set time intervals and choose the type of chart. You can also add technical indicators or compare several currency pairs on a single chart. The following websites have free online pricing charts:

- DailyFX.com (**www.dailyfx.com/charts**)
- ForexPros.com (**www.forexpros.com/charts**)

Line charts

The easiest charts to read are line charts, which show price data as a line on a graph, with the price data on the y-axis and the time interval on the x-axis. Line charts give a broad picture of the market and are helpful in identifying trends.

Line Chart

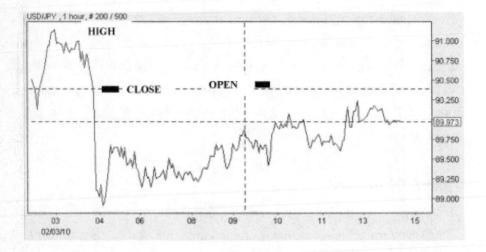

Bar charts

Bar charts are the most widely used type of chart in technical analysis. These charts are easy to construct and understand. In bar charts, market activity is represented in daily, weekly, or monthly intervals as vertical bars. Opening and closing prices are represented by vertical marks to the right and left of the vertical bars, respectively. Determining market patterns and trends on bar charts is easy and straightforward. Bar charts provide a method of displaying individual price data elements within a single time interval, without having to link with neighboring data.

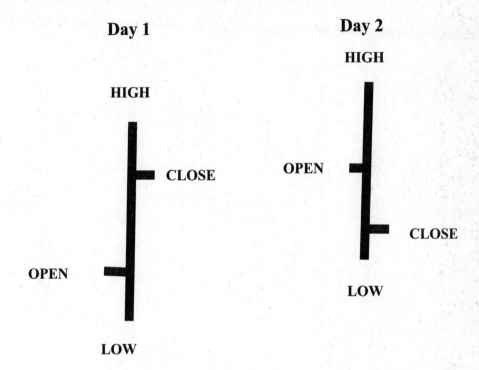

Each bar represents the price field for a single unit of time. The highest and lowest prices for the chosen time interval are indicated by the upper and lower boundaries of the charted bar, respectively. A horizontal rectangle jutting out from the left side of the bar represents the opening price for the chosen time period. The horizontal rectangle jutting out from the right side of the bar represents the closing price for the chosen time period. A typical open/high/low/close (OHLC) bar chart is shown below. The x-axis represents the chosen time interval, and the y-axis represents price.

Typical OHLC Bar Chart

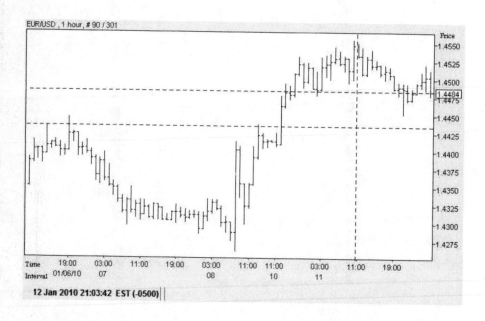

The horizontal rectangles provide a visual display of the relationship between opening and closing prices within a certain time. A bull or bear may be easily recognized for each time interval of the charted data. In a bull market, the closing price (rectangle extends left) is higher than the opening price (rectangle extends right). In a bear market, the opening price is higher than the closing price.

The charting packages offered by forex software and online forex brokers typically have more elaborate features, such as the use of colored bars to highlight specific types of activity. Real-time price data is continually charted as it comes in, and historical data is available for comparison and for analysis of long-term trends. The accuracy of the charts depends on the data feeds used by the broker. A trader can adjust the time interval on a bar chart to show price data over a period of years, months, days, hours, and even minutes.

Candlestick charting

Candlestick charting, which was developed in Japan in the 1700s as a method for charting rice trading, uses solid or empty bar fills to illustrate the ups and downs of market data. This charting method effectively illustrates highs, lows, opening, and closing prices over a specified time. The effects are thought to be more illuminating and dramatic than standard bar charts.

Candlestick Bars

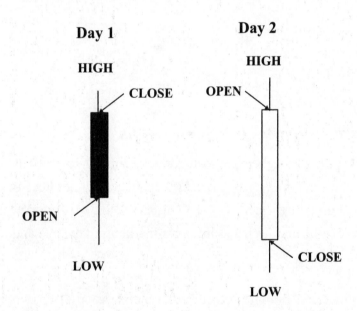

A candlestick bar is composed of a body and two shadows. The upper and lower boundaries of the body are the opening and closing prices. The body fill of the body is empty in a bull market — the closing price is higher than the opening price. The body fill is solid in a bear market — the closing price is lower than the opening price. Some candlestick charts use two colors for the bodies instead. Shadows or lines extend above and below the body. The upper shadow indicates the high price for the day, and the lower shadow indicates the low price for the day. The following is a typical candlestick chart follows.

Candlestick Chart

Common patterns in technical analysis

Technical analysts analyze, label, and categorize recurring formations in bar charts, in an effort to identify patterns that accurately predict future market behavior. These patterns are then correlated with market data and economic indicators to try to interpret market movements and trends.

Certain patterns that can be detected in price charts are well-known predictors of market movement. Trading strategies can be developed to recognize these patterns and take advantage of the expected price movements. Historically no system has proved to be 100 percent successful, and those that are accurate for a time lose their effectiveness when the market shifts.

Common formations include lines of support and resistance, head and shoulders patterns, triangular patterns, wedge patterns, channel patterns, and flag and pennant patterns.

Support and resistance

All market data shows points of support and resistance, and much market activity tends to occur around these points. Traders use support and resistance in determining the placement of stop-loss and profit limit orders. Support and resistance levels are shown on the bar chart below:

Support and Resistance

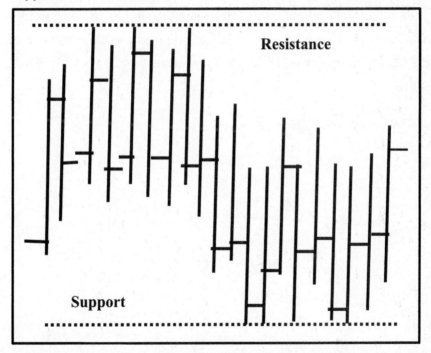

Support is a price point below the current market price in which buying reverses a downward trend. Support represents the price at which most traders expect prices to move higher. Support levels are characterized by a sequence of daily lows that fluctuate only slightly along a horizontal line. Support has many buyers. When a price drops below the support level, the support level is said to be "penetrated." At that point, a support level may become a resistance level. Traders will attempt to limit their losses and sell when prices approach the former level.

Resistance is a price point above the current market price in which selling reverses an upward trend. Resistance represents the price at which sellers typically outnumber buyers. When a resistance level is penetrated, price moves above the resistance level.

Head and shoulders pattern

Head and shoulders is a well-known reversal pattern that is most often seen in market uptrends. It occurs when the supply and demand for a particular currency achieve a balance, and portrays the behavior of speculating buyers and sellers when they suspect a currency price will soon drop.

Head and Shoulders Pattern

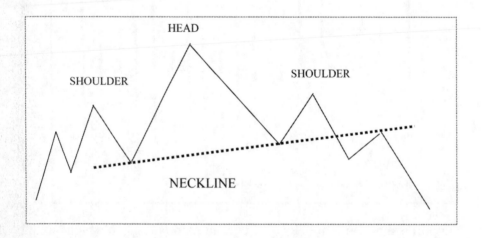

Peaks of the pattern are used to define the shoulders and head.

- **Left shoulder**: The market rises to a certain point, and sellers begin to exit the market, causing the price to drop.

- **Head**: The price drops low enough that buyers enter the market in large numbers, pushing the price much higher than before. At the high point, sellers exit and the price drops again.

- **Right shoulder**: The drop in price triggers more buying and the market rises slightly, then falls again in a shape similar to that of the left shoulder and continues a downward trend.

- **Neckline**: The line defined by the troughs on either side of the head.

Symmetrical triangle pattern

The symmetrical triangle pattern is a continuation pattern in which market data can be encapsulated in a right triangle, as shown below.

Symmetrical Triangle

UPTREND

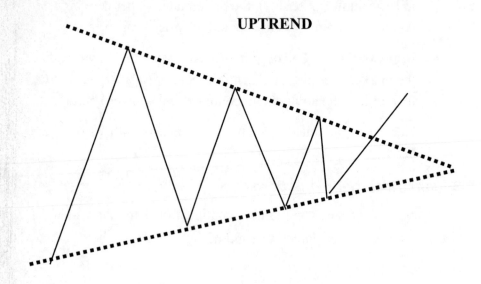

DOWNTREND

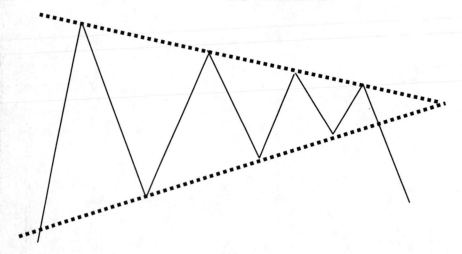

When the triangle formed is a descending right angle triangle, the pattern favors an upward trend. When the triangle is an ascending right angle triangle, the pattern favors a downward trend. If a line drawn through the troughs of the data forms the base of the triangle, it indicates that declines are deeper than gains. Symmetrical triangles represent indecision in the market; supply and demand have reached equilibrium and it is unclear which direction the market will take. The data encapsulated in the triangle indicates that the price dropped, and buyers sensed the commodity would be oversold. Buyers then entered the market and pushed the price upward. Sellers saw the gain and sold for profit, pushing the price back down. When the price fell, buyers reentered the market and pushed the price up again. In response, sellers sold and pushed the price down again in a repeating pattern. The price rises and falls less with each fluctuation, and the volume at such times tends to be low, favoring sellers. Eventually, buyers become decisive about the market and the price bursts out of the triangle formation, often with heavy volume. Research shows that triangle formations almost always resolve in the direction of the overall trend.

Wedge pattern

The wedge pattern is a continuation pattern very similar to the symmetrical triangle pattern. Trend lines drawn through the peaks and troughs intersect to form an angle. The angle will point either upward or downward, representing either a bull or bear trend, respectively. Typical wedge patterns are shown in the following chart.

Falling Wedge Pattern in a Downtrend Followed by a Reversal

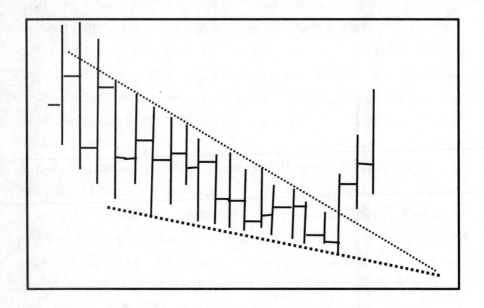

Rising Wedge Pattern in an Uptrend

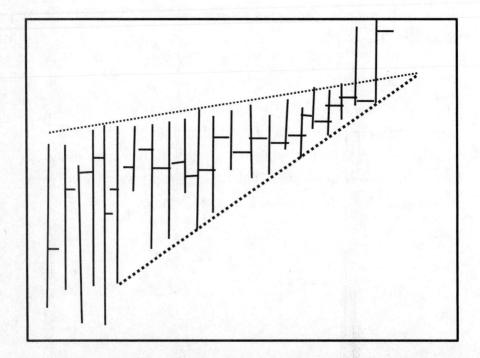

Like the symmetrical triangle, a wedge pattern represents a period when buyers are indecisive before a definitive price movement occurs.

Channel pattern

The channel pattern is a continuation pattern that usually represents indecision in the market. Trend lines drawn through peaks and troughs are generally flat during periods of low volume. The pattern itself typically does not follow the larger trend.

Channel Pattern

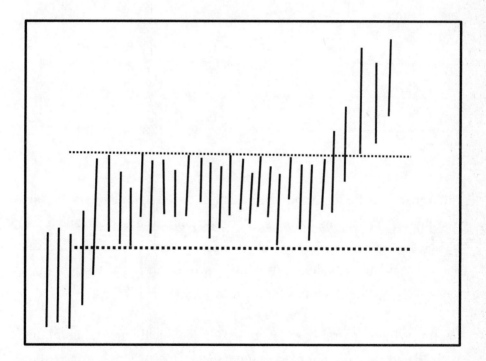

Flag and pennant patterns

Flag and pennant patterns are also continuation patterns representing periods of indecision, usually after big moves in currency prices have occurred. In the flag pattern, trend lines drawn through peaks typically parallel those drawn through troughs. In a pennant, the lines drawn through peaks and troughs intersect. A currency generally pauses at the flag or pennant pattern, and then resumes the direction it was heading before the pause. The shapes of a flag and a pennant pattern are shown in the following graphic.

Flag and Pennant Patterns

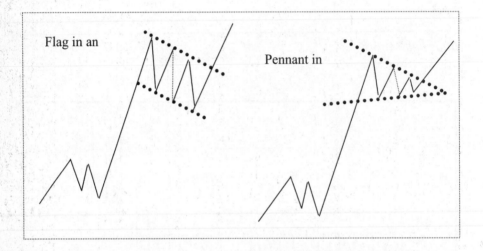

Price charts can be set to show price data at different time intervals, such as minutes, ticks, hours, or days. All of the patterns described above can be detected in data using any time interval. A chart set at short intervals shows many minor fluctuations in price, while charts set at longer intervals give a broader picture of price movement.

Currency trading strategies are based on technical analysis combined with an understanding of market fundamentals, but there is more to currency trading than simply watching price movements and placing buy and sell orders. *The next chapter describes some of the skills necessary for success.*

Chapter 7

The Mechanics of Forex

The advertisements on forex websites proclaiming that currency trading is simple and easy are exciting but also misleading. Individual forex traders share the global market with millions of other investors, banks, central banks, portfolio managers, and international financial institutions. Successful currency trading requires time, an understanding of the market, and a certain amount of self-restraint. You will often see a disclaimer of this type on forex websites: "Currency trading involves considerable risk. The foreign exchange market is a volatile market that does not guarantee a consistent profit. Trading forex is speculative and can easily result in loss." The use of high margins in forex trading increases the volatility of the market and the risk of large losses. Currency traders are cautioned to trade only with money they can realistically afford to lose. Trading can be mentally challenging and addictive to some people in the same way that gambling is addictive.

Currency traders must invest considerable time in their trades. The forex market does not have well-defined periods of time when the most beneficial trades can be made. Price movements can occur at any time during the 24-hour period for which the market is open, and must be carefully watched. Traders cannot enter a trade, go about other business, and still expect to make a profit.

Successful forex traders are able to analyze both fundamental and technical aspects of the market. Then, they make informed decisions based on their perceptions of the sensitivity and expectations of the market. This requires staying abreast of market conditions around the globe, educating oneself about the market, and checking various news outlets to monitor changes in the market. Timing is also important — even the most successful traders sometimes experience off timing. Successful traders recognize that money management and psychology play an important role in the trading process. They do not expect to generate a return on every single trade. There are, however, some practices traders can use to increase the probability of engaging in profitable trades.

TIP: Forex trading requires more than analysis and strategy.

Fundamental and technical analyses are not the only components of a good trading system. Psychology and money management play a vital role in trading decisions. Analyses provide information and indicators to define entry and exit points, but psychology and poor money management can cause you to fail to respond appropriately. Though most traders devote their time to developing a trading strategy, the most successful traders insist that strategy is the least important component, and forex traders would do better to focus more on psychology and money management.

Money Management

Success in currency trading depends on two skills: good money management and the ability to determine the best point at which to enter and exit a trade. Most trading strategies establish when a trade should be entered, but some strategies do not establish an exit. If a strategy does not provide exit points, you must decide on a method for determining when to exit, and then establish your own entry and exit points.

Profit and loss (P/L)

In any type of investment, it is necessary to keep track of your gains and losses so that you know whether you are succeeding and achieving your goals. Forex trading provides one of the easiest forms of executing trades and monitoring profit and loss (P/L). P/Ls in the spot market are generally measured in decimal units. For example, the value of USD/ GBP is 1.4536 at the open of trading. A trader buys one standardized lot, leveraged 100:1. The long position is calculated as follows:

$100,000 x 1.4536 = 145,360 British pounds

At the close of trade USD/GBP is 1.4542 and the trader sells a standardized lot. The short position is calculated as follows:

$100,000 x 1.4542 = 145,420 British pounds

The trader sells the unit for more than it was bought.
The position profits as follows:

145,420 pounds – 145,360 pounds = 60 British pounds

The profit from this trade equates to U.S. dollars as follows:

1.4542 British pounds = 1 dollar

60 British pounds = 60 ÷ 1.4542

$41.26

Gains to losses: Determining how much to invest

Every currency trader experiences losses on some trades; the key is to ensure that profit from successful trades (gains) exceeds losses from losing trades. The ratio of gains to losses assists in determining how much a trader should invest in a particular currency trade.

The trader must determine how large a percentage of winning trades to expect and have some method for predicting the chances of winning. If trades are providing a high percentage of wins, and a higher percentage of gains than losses, an investor need not invest more money in winning trades. It might be unrealistic to expect 85 percent wins with a 10:1 ratio of gains to losses, but most traders would find 30 percent wins with a

5:1 ratio acceptable. Some traders, however, expect a 1:1 ratio and need about 60 percent wins to be able to stay in the trading game.

Limiting losses

Traders limit their losses by establishing take-profit and stop-limit orders close to the market price used on entry into the market. A stop-loss limit means that you will automatically sell the currency pair if the price drops to a certain level. A take-profit limit is the price at which you will automatically sell a currency pair when its price is rising, to preserve your profit and prevent losses if the price suddenly drops again. By raising stop-limit orders to just below the market entry price, and lowering take-profit orders, traders can reduce potential losses. If, soon after a purchase order has been placed, it becomes clear the prices are not going to rise as expected, a trader can eliminate any further potential loss by manually liquidating the trade, before the price reaches the stop-order limit. If, on the other hand, the price moves are more favorable than expected, a trader might raise the limits of both take-profit and stop-limit orders. When the price rises rapidly, a stop-limit order can be raised above the market-entry price, to guarantee a profit of at least the difference between the market price and the newly established stop-limit price.

A trader in a long position should avoid lowering stop-limit orders. It is better to accept a loss and possibly engage in the trade of a different currency pair than to risk losing even more. Take-profit orders should only be lowered in long positions if a possible reversal is anticipated. If the trader believes there is a strong probability of a reversal, it is better to liquidate and take a profit before the price falls. Likewise, in short positions, traders should avoid increasing stop-limit orders and only increase take-profit orders in anticipation of a reversal. Moving and removing stop-loss orders usually causes large losses in either long or short positions.

Stop-loss orders are typically placed below and above previous highs or lows. However, it may be advantageous to set such stops according to market volatility. Examine recent charts for traded currency pairs and determine the average of sub-trends of the major and minor trend directions. These averages should be determined periodically to gauge any shift in volatility. The information should then be used to set stops and price objectives. This method may also be used to establish entry points in the market.

Risk/reward ratio

Many traders have a tendency to focus on the rewards of trading, considering the amount of risk involved. The risk/reward ratio is a measure of risk taken compared to reward received. Most risk/reward ratios list the reward first. A ratio of 5:1 indicates the reward is five times greater than the risk.

The risk/reward ratio can be calculated by dividing a take-profit spread by a corresponding stop-limit spread. For example, a trader seeks a risk/reward ratio of 3:1 and takes a long position in JPY/USD based on a fundamental analysis. The current price for JPY/USD is 1.500 and an analysis suggests that the price will increase to JPY/USD 1.650 within the next 24 hours. No rollover or interest rate differential enters into this calculation because the entire transaction will occur within the same 24-hour period. To achieve the 3:1 risk/reward ratio, the trader must set a take-profit order at 1.650 and a stop-limit order at 1.450:

Take-profit spread = 1.650 − 1.500 = 150 pips

Stop-limit spread = 1.500 − 1.450 = 50 pips

The risk/reward ratio is calculated as follows:

Take-profit spread /stop-limit spread

= 150/50   = 3:1

If the price rises to 1.650 and the take-profit order is executed, the trader will gain a profit of 150 pips. However, if the price dips soon after the order is placed, and the stop-limit order is executed first, the trader loses 50 pips. If 1 pip = $100, the profit and loss would be as follows:

$$Profit = 150 \text{ pips} \times \$100 = \$15,000$$
$$Loss = 50 \text{ pips} \times \$100 = \$5,000$$

TIP: Never commit more than 10 percent of your total investment capital to a single trade.

Never allocate more than 10 percent of your total investment capital to a single trade, as either margin or risk. You should also have enough investment capital available to engage in 30 to 50 different trades. If some trades result in losses, you have a good chance of recovering those losses with other trades. If half or more or your trades result in loss, analyze and adjust your trading strategy.

Psychology

Forex trading requires emotional detachment. Losses are inevitable, and should not be allowed to become the cause of emotional stress or physical illness. Forex traders are also cautioned against becoming overconfident. A profitable trade, especially for a novice trader, may lead him or her to engage in more trades than can be reasonably tracked in a trading session. Moderation, experience, and intuition help a trader know when to take calculated risks to succeed in trading. A successful forex trader has control over his or her emotions. Being overly excited about a win or depressed over a loss only impedes a trader's ability to think clearly.

Self-analysis

The first step in developing a trading strategy is to determine whether forex is an appropriate investment for you.

Ask yourself:

- How well do I understand this investment?

- Am I fully aware of the risks involved?

- Am I prepared to dedicate the time and energy necessary to make sound decisions?

- Does this investment fit within my portfolio and investment objectives?

If you do not answer these questions honestly, there is a good possibility you will lose money in currency trading. The risk associated with forex is high and should be reserved for investors who are able to absorb losses that may multiply as the market jumps and dives. It is not a good investment for those with modest incomes and savings.

TIP: Avoid the two most common mistakes.

The two most common mistakes new investors make are not having a plan and attempting to trade against the market. Trading by instinct almost always guarantees a loss. Investors who cannot explain why they are trading and what they intend to do, in the event they realize either a profit or a loss, do not have a plan. Hoping that a trade shows a profit is not considered having a plan. Another common mistake is trading against the market. An investor who has suffered a loss may decide to invest more, with the expectation that the market will rebound and losses will be recovered. Though this might be a possibility, it is not probable enough to rely on. Instead, an investor should cut losses by getting out of the market when the position takes a loss. A profitable position should be maintained until it hits the intended target.

Developing a Trading Strategy

Trading strategies emerge over time. Each strategy begins with the selection of a currency pair to be traded. You then take a position to buy or sell the currency, select the number of units to trade, and initiate a trade. There are two options for initiating a trade: a market order or a limit order. A market order allows a trade to be executed at the current market price. A limit order delays the execution of the trade until the market price reaches the predetermined limit you have established.

To safeguard the investment, you also need to set stop-loss and take-profit limits. The establishment of stop-loss and take-profit limits is subjective, based on your sensitivity to risk. Some trading platforms will automatically calculate these values for you, either as a percentage of the current trading range or as a linear distance from the market entry price. Linear distances of ten, 20, or 25 pips are calculated on both sides of the entry price. Traders in open positions have the option of using the calculated values or adjusting them. Stop-loss and take-profit orders are especially important in online trading. The market could hit a trader's limit or a price could revert to or below the market price in the time it takes you to reboot your computer after a crash, restore your Internet connection, or recover from a power failure.

Establish a plan

Forex trading should be treated as a business and not as a hobby. Do not just hope for the best; prepare for all possibilities with a plan that includes contingencies. You must be prepared to accept losses, but never ride on a losing trade or add to a losing trade. Though some traders consider themselves to be fundamental traders and others consider themselves to be technical traders, based on the type of analysis used, a mix of both types of analysis is necessary for successful trading. Any available, valid market data should be used in an analysis, regardless of the particular discipline used in generating or gathering the data. An analysis is subjective, and the amount of weight to be given to either discipline will ultimately be determined from experience. Be prepared to make adjustments to, but not change, your trading style. A strategy may need to be modified, but should never be completely changed, just because a single trade went wrong.

Establish positions

When a chosen position moves unfavorably, you have two options: allow the price action to trigger automatic liquidation of the order; or manually liquidate the position before the stop-loss is triggered, if you perceive the price direction will not reverse itself. Lowering a stop-loss order in a long position, with the expectation that a dropping price will reverse for a short period of time and let you exit more favorably before moving down again, is not recommended, because the odds are against this type of price movement.

If a chosen position moves favorably, you have many options, depending on price volatility. A significant move of 15 to 20 pips in a long position is a signal to move the stop-loss limit above the market entry price by about 3 to 5 pips and raise the take-profit limit by about 20 pips. If the price continues to move favorably, keep raising the stop-loss and take-profit limits, locking in guaranteed profits while the market runs its course. The take-profit limit should not be allowed to trigger an exit from the trade. Instead, market exit should be the result of a reversal that triggers the favorably adjusted stop-loss limit order. The only exception is when the trader feels it is necessary to exit the trade manually.

TIP: Evaluate the distance between your stop-loss and take-profit limits.

You should feel comfortable with how close the two limit orders are set in relation to the current price. By determining support and resistance lines for the price immediately preceding a current price, you can get a feel for the range of trading in the immediate past.

Pyramiding

The process of adding to a favorable open position by initiating new orders in the same currency pair and in the same position is called pyramiding. Experienced traders handle pyramiding best, because they are able to monitor margin requirements and track the balance of their margin accounts. A margin account can quickly become overdrawn or liquidated when a sharp, unfavorable reversal occurs if new orders have been initiated for trades from unrealized profits.

Analyze the market

Most traders use both fundamental and technical analysis in developing their own trading strategies. A general principle of forex trading is that the most highly traded currency pairs, such as the G8, tend to move technically, and the more exotic currency pairs tend to follow more fundamental behaviors. However, a combination of both technical and fundamental trading strategies, and a good understanding of the market, are necessary for success.

> **TIP: Begin by trading with the major currencies.**
>
> Novice traders should begin by trading with the major currencies, particularly those currency pairs that include USD. These currency pairs usually have lower transaction costs and lower bid/ask spreads that increases profit potential.

Determine volatility and liquidity

Because the forex market is open 24 hours a day, it is impossible for an individual to track all market movements or to respond to movements at all times; however, timing is very important to currency trading. An effective and time-efficient trading strategy relies on an awareness of global market activity to maximize the trading opportunities available, during the hours when a currency trader is active.

Volatility is the amount a currency price fluctuates (ranges) during a given time period. All currency pairs experience higher volatility at certain times of the day and under certain market conditions. A currency pair's trading range is affected by geographical location and macroeconomic factors. A trader needs to know what times of day a particular currency pair experiences its widest or narrowest trading ranges, in order to allocate investment capital most effectively. Traders should become familiar with the trading activities of currency pairs in different time zones and know the times when those pairings are most volatile.

Liquidity is the volume of trades for a particular currency pair. A highly liquid currency pair, such as USD/EUR, can be quickly bought and sold in large quantities. During periods of low volume, buy and sell orders for a thinly traded currency pair may not be fulfilled immediately, increasing the risk that prices will be requoted before the order is completed.

European trading session

The London market offers such high liquidity and efficiency that the majority of foreign exchange transactions are completed during the London market hours — 2 a.m. to 12 p.m. EST. Vast numbers of market participants and large individual transactions make the London market the most volatile foreign exchange market in the world. London has the largest and most important currency dealing center, which accounts for about 30 percent of all currency trading. Most of the dealing desks of large banks are located in London.

A price range of 80 pips is the benchmark used for establishing a currency pair as volatile. During the London session, six major currency pairs typically average price ranges of more than 80 pips. The GBP/CHF and GBP/JPY pairs experience average daily ranges of more than

140 pips, and appeal to traders with high risk tolerance because they can be used to generate large profits in short amounts of time. This high volatility is due to the peak in daily trade activities that occurs when large market participants complete their cycle of currency conversions around the globe. There is a direct connection between London trading hours and U.S. and Asian trading hours. As large banks and institutional investors finish repositioning their investment portfolios for the day or week, they need to convert their European assets into dollar-dominated assets in anticipation of the U.S. market opening. These conversions by the big market participants are responsible for the extreme volatility in the GBP/CHF and GBP/JPY pairs.

The four pairs, USD/CHF, GBP/USD, USD/CAD, and EUR/USD, have an average range of 100 pips. Their high volatility provides traders with a number of opportunities to enter the market.

Currency pairs that average about 50 pips promise high potential profit as well as interest income. Investors can anticipate the direction of movements based on fundamental economic factors, making them less prone to losses from intraday speculative trades.

U.S. trading session

The New York trading session is between 8 a.m. and 5 p.m. EST. The majority of its transactions occur between 8 a.m. and noon when the European market is still in session and liquidity is high. New York has the second largest foreign exchange market in the world.

During the U.S. trading session, the daily ranges of the GBP/CHF, GBP/JPY, USD/CHF, and GBP/USD pairs average about 120 pips, due to transactions directly involving the U.S. dollar. Foreign investors must convert their domestic currencies to dollar-dominated assets in order to participate in the U.S. equity and bond markets.

Most currencies in the foreign exchange market are quoted in U.S. dollars, usually the base currency. These currencies are then traded against the U.S. dollar before being translated into other currencies. In the case of GBP/CHF, the British pound is traded against the U.S. dollar and then converted to Swiss francs. The trade involves two transactions, GBP/USD and USD/CHF. Volatility is determined by the correlation of the two derived currency pairs, a measure of how closely the two currencies move in the same direction. A negative correlation signifies that the currencies are moving in opposite directions. (If GBP/USD and USD/CHF have negative correlations, the volatility of GBP/CHF is increased.) Highly volatile currency pairs offer a high profit potential, but are also associated with high risk. Traders must continually respond to market conditions and revise their strategies because abrupt movements in exchange rates can potentially stop their trading orders or nullify long-term strategies.

The USD/CAD, EUR/USD, and USD/JPY offer a wide enough range to make a profit with a smaller amount of risk. Because they are highly liquid, investors can take profits or cut their losses immediately and efficiently. Their modest volatility allows traders to pursue long-term strategies.

Asian trading session

Foreign exchange trades during the Asian trading session occur between 7 p.m. and 4 a.m. EST. Trades are conducted in regional financial hubs, with Tokyo having the largest market share. Hong Kong and Singapore have the second- and third-largest share, respectively. The BOJ has a strong influence on the foreign exchange market, and Tokyo is one of the most important dealing centers. Some market participants use the trade momentum of the Tokyo market to gauge market dynamics and devise trading strategies. Hedge funds and large investment banks may use the Asian session to implement stops and option barrier limits.

During the Asian trading session, the GBP/JPY, GBP/CHF, and USD/JPY pairs experience the broadest range, typically averaging about 90 pips. The three pairs — USD/CHF, GBP/USD, and AUD/JPY — appeal to medium- to long-term traders because these trades allow traders to factor fundamentals into their decision-making. The moderate volatility of these pairs helps shield traders and their strategies from potentially irregular market movement resulting from intraday speculative trades.

Institutional investors and foreign investment banks generate a significant volume of USD/JPY transactions, because these banks position themselves to enter the Japanese bond and equity markets. The majority of assets held by these financial entities is dollar-dominated and must be converted into Japanese yen before entering the Japanese markets. Through its open market operations, the BOJ has an influential role in the supply and demand of USD/JPY. The central bank holds more than $573.2 billion in U.S. Treasury securities. Large Japanese exporters who also need to convert their foreign earnings play a role in increasing the volume of USD/JPY transactions during the Tokyo trading hours.

GBP/CHF and GBP/JPY are highly volatile, because big market participants and central bankers take positions in anticipation of the opening of the European session.

Trading session overlaps

The foreign exchange market tends to be more active when markets overlap, particularly when the two largest trading centers, United States and European, overlap. Market overlaps between the United States and European sessions and the European and Asian sessions are shown in the table below, with the dark gray shading indicating the overlap.

US-European-Asian Trading Session Overlaps

EST	AM							PM												AM					
	6	7	8	9	10	11	12	1	2	3	4	5	6	7	8	9	10	11	12	1	2	3	4	5	6
U.S.			▓	▓	▓	▓	▓	▓	▓	▓	▓	▓													
European	▓	▓	▓	▓	▓	▓	▓														▓	▓	▓		
Asian												▓	▓	▓	▓	▓	▓	▓	▓	▓	▓	▓	▓		

United States-European trading sessions overlap

Trading between 8 a.m. and noon EST, a period referred to by currency traders as the power hours, accounts, on average, for 70 percent of the average trading for all currency pairs during the European session; and 80 percent of the average trading for all currency pairs during the U.S. session. Day traders who seek wide ranges and volatile price actions find this to be a good time to trade.

European-Asian trading session overlap

Trading volume between 2 a.m. and 4 a.m. EST, a period referred to as the cold zone, is lower than any other trading session because of slow trading during the early Asian trading hours. Risk tolerant traders typically ignore these thin trading hours or use the time to position themselves for a breakout move when the U.S. or European markets open.

Determine trends

As part of a trading strategy, you must be able to evaluate the market and determine whether trends are moving upward or downward; are weakening or strengthening; are newly formed or long standing; or are in a good trading range. Successful traders do not categorize the price of a trade as "too high" or "too low" — they consider the price of one currency relative to another and try to maintain a clear picture of market situations.

No matter how complex or how simple your trading system, you can benefit from charted market data. Charts provide insight into trends and time series ranges. Trends in the market are best recognized by studying charts of market data. You must understand and be able to interpret charted data because different trends can be observed on charts of the same data when differing scales are applied. Some important indicators in charted data include the length of primary versus secondary trends, average times between trend tops and bottoms, and the average range charted over various time intervals. Charting data for the same market, on different scales, also provides a good perspective on market trends. Data charted over minutes or hours can provide a much different perspective from data charted daily. Price movement and volatility may also be charted.

After you have identified a trend, you must determine what you will do if prices open higher or lower than expected, if the market is quiet or volatile, if the market experiences new highs or new lows, and if the market experiences highs or lows early and then reverses.

Chapter 8

Trading Strategies

Each trader develops a trading approach that embodies his or her personality and trading behaviors. A good approach allows the trader to pinpoint flaws in a strategy and make adjustments quickly while continuing to trade successfully.

The inverted pyramid is a classic approach model used for evaluating the risks associated with specific trades. Most traders, brokers, and dealers follow this approach to trading, either consciously or instinctively. After selecting a currency pair, the trader first considers all macroeconomic factors of the trade (the top of the inverted pyramid). Then, moving down the inverted pyramid, he or she considers all of the technical factors, until arriving at specific entry and exit points at the bottom of the pyramid. Traders may assign weight to the different parts of the pyramid depending on their strategies. For example, purely technical traders may apply more weight to the bottom of the pyramid, and fundamental traders give more weight to the top of the inverted pyramid.

The following is a graphic representation of an inverted pyramid.

Inverted Pyramid Trading Strategy

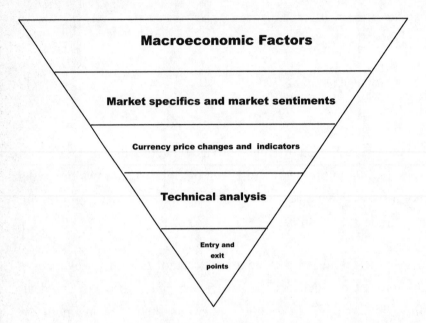

- First, the macroeconomic factors to be considered at the top of the inverted pyramid provide a broad overview of international issues, including factors that influence the global trading community, such as the extent of global terrorism, oil price fluctuations, and possibilities of war. Most macro indicators can be derived from credible news feeds and TV news with world coverage, such as CNN or BBC.

- Second, a trader considers market specifics and market sentiment. Market specifics include specifics of the currency markets. The trader determines what events are significant enough to affect markets and establish trading behavior for the particular market. Market sentiment incorporates the general feel surrounding the market. Analyst market reports and news reports provide the best picture of the market and its direction. A trader should be able to develop a complete picture of the market at this stage before moving further down the inverted triangle.

- Next, the trader considers currency price changes and indicators to identify currency pairs that are volatile in the macro environment and market conditions, identified during the first two stages. Traders should understand which indicators are significant and which activities represent non-events. They must determine whether price movements clearly represent a trend or if spikes in price movement are simply a result of volatility. After this analysis, the trader should focus on potential trades between the most probable currency pairs.

- The fourth step of this approach involves evaluating the basic technology of the trade. Floors and ceilings established by technical analysis provide traders with valid psychological trading levels, and traders tend to sit on these levels. Technical patterns allow traders to formulate views on the direction of specific currency pairs. After a currency pair is selected, its market sentiment should then be re-examined in light of the technical analysis.

- Finally, a trader determines micro indicators, fine-tuning trading strategy by identifying entry and exit points to be used in executing trades. Traders must determine the type of technical indicators that are most effective for their strategies. Some traders use chance and randomness in their strategy, but others prefer weighted moving averages.

CASE STUDY:
ADVICE FROM AN EXPERT

Mark L. Waggoner, President
Excel Futures, Inc.
16691 Gothard Street, Suite #L
Huntington Beach, CA. 92647
www.excelfutures.com
Toll Free: (888) 959-9955
International: 01-714-843-9884

Mark Waggoner is the President of Excel Futures in Huntington Beach, Calif., and has been trading since 1990. He publishes a daily and weekly trade advisory: The Trade Accord *and* The TrendTracker. *Mr. Waggoner is frequently a guest on Bloomberg Television and Radio and provides market commentary to Reuters and CNBC.*

What was a particularly interesting, successful experience you have had in currency trading?

In 2000-2004 rates in the United States were dropping. Major currencies rallied as the U.S. dollar drifted lower. This is the classic example of following interest rates. Thousands could have been made over the course of two or three years.

What are the steps one must take to enter currency trading?

First and foremost, do your homework. I like to look at which countries are raising rates (buy) and which are lowering rates (sell). Look for established trends. There is not really a whole lot to it if you are playing long-term trends. If you are playing short term, it becomes much more complicated and will require more homework.

Does a currency trader need to be in a large city, or can anyone with an Internet connection enter the field?

Anyone with an Internet connection will be able to trade. I do not even suggest trading without it because you need the frequently updated news and information. It's much faster than television or newspapers.

Which currencies traditionally do well when traded?

Any major currencies can be traded. To start, stay with the most common.

What would you advise someone who is just starting out as a currency trader?

Watch trends and buy if a market is going up; sell if the market is going down.

How much of an investment would you recommend that a person have on hand before launching a currency trading business?

We recommend a minimum of $10,000. Statistically your chances of making money are dramatically increased. Remember *always* leave 50 percent of your funds on the sideline for adverse price movement and *always* use stops.

Is there is anything else you would like to mention that would be helpful?

Wait for trades to come to you. Most trades will present themselves. Just because you opened an account does not mean you have to trade that day. Check, recheck, and then enter a market. Have a plan that is written for each trade that includes: Entry Point, Stop, Exit Strategy

When the trade is right, you will know and enter the market.

Parameters

Every market can be defined using volatility and price movement, or trend slope. Volatility is a measure of how much and how often a price changes over time. Price movement is a measure of the slope of the trend from some defined beginning to end point. All market activity can be defined by its charted position on scales of both volatility and price movement. Market conditions also play a role in market activity, because a shift in conditions can change a market.

A trading environment has two elements — a schedule and the three-chart system. The schedule includes the period of time between when the trader plans to get into the market and when he or she plans to get out of the market. Traders extrapolate expected price movements to arrive at price evolutions during specified periods of time. Traders need to establish entry prices and exit prices without being able to predict exactly when to exit the market.

The decision whether to trade for a day or trade for the long term determines the schedule for charting data. A trader who engages in many trades in a one-day period will find it more beneficial to analyze data that describe market activity over minutes or hours, rather than data charted by days. It is also beneficial to recognize those times when various financial entities enter and exit the market because any volatility and liquidity experienced during these times influences market movement.

The three-chart system uses charts with three different deadlines to determine entry and exit in the market. Different traders include differing scales of charted data in their trading systems — scalpers are more likely to use ticks, day traders are more likely to use short intervals of minutes, and position traders are more likely to use longer intervals of minutes, as shown in the following timing matrix.

Timing Matrix for Traders

Trader	Timing	Home	Trend
Scalper	Tick	1-5 minutes	1 hour
Day Trader	1 minute	5-10 minutes	1 day
Position Trader	10 minutes	1-24 hours	2 days

A trader must decide the level of trading that he or she plans to use, established in the timing matrix as home. Because forex markets offer leverage and are often volatile, very few traders establish home as more than one day. Once a trader has determined the particular currency pair to trade and the market entry price, he or she must then decide other parameters for a trade. These parameters include trade unit size, duration, stop loss-order differential, and take-profit order differential. They are defined as the following:

- **Trade unit size**: Trade unit size is only applicable when traders are allowed to trade odd lot sizes. It is recommended that small traders invest no more than 10 percent of their margin accounts in a single trade.

- **Duration**: If a trader is trading in different currency pairs and a limit order is triggered, it will reduce the amount of margin available. Duration, or expiry, is the time that a trader requires a broker to keep an un-triggered limit order active. It is recommended that limit orders be held for a few hours or less than one day.

- **Stop-loss order differential**: A stop-loss order differential is the number of pips below the entry price that a stop-limit order is placed in a long trade and vice versa in a short trade.

- **Take-profit order differential**: A take-profit order differential is the number of pips above the entry price that a take-profit order is placed in a long trade and vice versa in a short trade.

Trading Matrices

A price matrix is a specific price fluctuation pattern that can be used to set entry and exit points for a profitable trade. When market actions match the pattern of the matrix, a trader can profit by entering the market when the price is at a low point and exiting when the price rises again. Price matrices may occur concurrently at different time intervals and on different scales. A price action has three consecutive legs. The first leg is the initial trend, which may be either upward or downward. The second leg retraces in the opposite direction. The final leg is a trend in the direction of the first leg.

Price Matrix

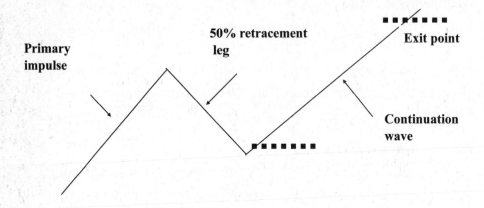

Each leg of a price matrix is scaled on the same time interval. Parameters must be established to determine what constitutes the "retracement" leg. Usually, a new leg is triggered when a minimum percentage of the preceding leg is reached or a minimum number of pips in the opposite direction is established.

Traders at any trading level can use the price matrix shown above. The level or time interval at which a trader is trading is his or her home level. Typically, traders should evaluate the market with their home levels first and then explore levels above and below their home levels. Evaluation of an above level (a level with a longer time interval) will give an idea of the overall market trend, and a below level (a level with a shorter time interval) should be used for timing entry, exit, and stop-loss orders.

Timing

Forex trading occurs in an exceptionally fast market that is naturally inconsistent. Timing and rhythms in forex are much harder to predict than the timing used in other markets, such as the stock market. Trading activity tends to correspond to the trading schedules of various cities around the globe. For example, trading tends to increase around 4 a.m.

EST, after the London market opens, and to decrease around 11 p.m. EST, which is when traders in the Tokyo market take a lunch break. It is likely to increase again at 8 a.m. when the U.S. market opens.

Activity of EUR/USD Price throughout the Day

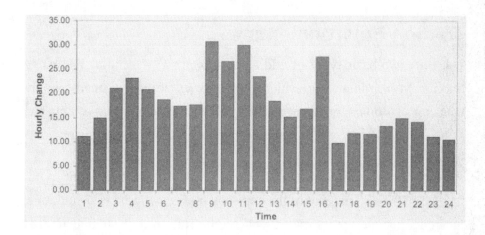

Some traders concentrate on trading during a specific time period when the price for a particular currency is volatile.

Performance Evaluations

It is helpful to keep a log of each day's trading performance. This need not be a cumbersome log of each and every trade, but a synopsis of each day's performance. Keeping an organized record of your trading activity will allow you to see which strategies have been the most successful, and what other factors might have contributed to profit or loss over time.

Performance Log

Date	Beginning Balance	Number of Trades	Pairs Traded	Strategies Used	Ending Balance	Comments
5/1/2011						
5/2/2011						

5/3/2011						
5/4/2011						
5/5/2011						
5/6/2011						
5/7/2011						

Trading Environments

There are two basic types of trading environment — trending and range trading. In trending, price fluctuations are exhibiting a steady movement up or down. In range trading, price fluctuations stay within the same upper and lower boundaries for an extended period of time.

At any given time in trade, a currency is either range trading or trending. More than 80 percent of the currency market volume is speculative, meaning currency pairs may spend a long time in a particular trading environment. Indicators show currencies sometimes follow trends, and at other times fall within specific ranges. Traders need to identify the environment in which they will be trading, and determine whether a market is trending or range bound by defining the appropriate trade parameters.

Some method must be used to determine which indicators to use in charted data, but no indicators are foolproof. A stochastic model is based on the premise that, as prices increase or decrease, closing prices tend to approximate more and more closely to the high or low prices for a given period. One stochastic strategy used by range traders involves buying when currencies are oversold and selling when they are overbought. Traders have been successful with this strategy, but when the market stops trading ranges and begins to follow trends, losses are almost guaranteed. A successful trader is able to adapt when the market changes.

Many traders assess market data visually to determine the environment. The following set of rules is also used to determine whether the market is ranging or trending:

Ranging and Trending Rules

Trading Environment	Rules	Indicators
Range	ADX less than 20	ADX Bollinger bands Options
	Decreasing volatility	
	Risk reversal near choice	
	Flipping between favoring calls and puts	
Trend	ADX greater than 25	ADX Momentum Moving averages Options
	Momentum consistent with direction of trend	
	Risk reversals bid for put or call	

Range rules:

- The average directional index (ADX) is one of the primary technical indicators used to determine the strength of a trend. The ADX was developed by J. Welles Wilder to measures the strength of market trends on a scale of 0 to 100. An ADX that is less than 20 indicates a weak trend, a major characteristic of a range-bound market. When the ADX is less than 20 on a weak downward trend, it indicates that the trend is very likely to stay in a range-trading environment for some time. Most charting packages include ADX.

- Volatility may be analyzed in many different ways. One method involves tracking short-term versus long-term volatility. When short-term volatility is falling, particularly a fall following a burst above long-term volatility, it usually indicates a reversion to range trading. Volatility usually expands with the sharp, quick movement of a currency pair and lessens when the trading is quiet and the ranges are narrow. Bollinger bands, introduced by John Bollinger in the 1980s, are a pair of trading bands or lines plotted on a chart to represent the predictable upper and lower limits of a trading range for a particular market price. A market price or currency pair is expected to trade within these upper and lower limits. The lines are plotted at standard deviation levels above and below the moving average. Bollinger bands may be used to track short- versus long-term volatility. Narrowed Bollinger bands usually indicate low volatility and small ranges, and widened Bollinger bands indicate a higher volatility and large ranges. As a result, in a range trading environment traders should seek relatively narrow Bollinger bands that are ideally in a horizontal position.

- A risk reversal is both a call and put option on the same currency. Risk reversals have an expiration and sensitivity the same as that of the underlying spot rate. The expiration date is one month. Risk reversals are quoted as the difference in volatility between the two options. In theory, the call and put options should have the same implied volatility. In practice, their volatilities often differ in the market. Risk reversals may be given a market polling function to gauge positions in the forex market. A value strongly in favor of calls over puts indicates that the market prefers calls over puts; a value that strongly favors puts over calls indicates that the market prefers puts to calls. In an ideal environment, far-reaching calls and puts should have the same volatility, but this is rarely the case because there is usually some sentiment in the market that is reflected in risk reversals. In a range market, risk reversal tends to flip between favoring calls and puts equal to or near zero, indicating that there is no strong bias in the markets and there is indecision among bulls and bears. In a range bound environment, risk reversals should near zero. A free resource that provides updated risk reversals can be found at FX.com (**www.fx.com**) using the IFR news plug-in.

Oscillators are technical tools that fluctuate between two parameters and are used to indicate the strength and direction of a trend. Three common oscillators are stochastics, parabolic stop and reversal (SAR), and the relative strength index (RSI). Stochastics measure when the market is overbought or oversold on a scale from 0 to 100. Stochastic lines above 80 indicate that the market is overbought. Stochastic lines below 20 indicate that the market is oversold. A parabolic SAR shows dots, or points, on a chart wherever there are potential reversals in price movement. During an uptrend, SAR is below market prices, and during a downtrend it shifts above the market prices. The RSI, like stochastics, indicates when the market is overbought or oversold on a scale of 0 to 100. Readings 30 or below, indicate the market is oversold, while readings 70 and above indicate the market is overbought.

Trend rules:

- When an ADX value is greater than 25, it indicates a trending environment, particularly when an ADX value is greater than 25 and rising. However, if the ADX value is greater than 25 but sloping downward off the extreme 40 level, it might indicate that the trend is fading.

- Momentum indicators should indicate that momentum is consistent with the direction of the trend. Oscillators should point in the direction of a trend. If the trend is upward, several oscillators should be examined and should all point upward. If the trend is downward, oscillators should point downward. Some traders may rely on the momentum index, but the strongest momentum indicator is a perfect order in moving averages.

In moving averages for an uptrend, for example, the ten-day simple moving average (SMA) is greater than the 20-day SMA, which is greater than the 50-day SMA. The 100-day and 200-day SMAs are below the shorter term moving averages. In a downtrend, perfect order is indicated when the shorter term moving averages fall below the longer term moving averages.

- Risk reversals should strongly favor puts and calls. When one side of the market has high interest rates, it usually indicates a strong trend environment. However, if risk reversals are at extreme levels, it may indicate that a trend reversal is on the horizon.

Moving average convergence/divergence (MACD) is calculated by subtracting a 12-day exponential moving average value from a 26-day exponential moving average value. When MACD increases, prices go up and when MACD decreases prices go down. When the MACD crosses a line plotted using a nine-day exponential average, it is a signal to buy or sell.

Fibonacci retracements are percentage measurements of the amount that individual price fluctuations reverse from an overall trend. These help traders to predict the next movement of a currency price and discover trend reversals. The three most commonly used Fibonacci ratios are 38.2 percent, 50 percent, and 61.8 percent. Many charting packages show Fibonacci retracements. (You can find a good demonstration on the Currency Trading USA website **www.currencytradingusa.com/fibonacci.htm**).

Elliott wave analysis is based on the principle that market prices reflect the mass psychology of the market and recur in predictable patterns, known as Elliott Waves. Elliott wave patterns move up in a sequence of five waves and down in a pattern of three waves. Elliott waves are used to predict price movements during trends.

Ichimoku clouds, developed by a Japanese journalist, use five lines to gauge a trend's momentum, along with future areas of support and resistance.

Once a trader determines whether the trading environment is range bound or trending, he or she must decide how long to hold a particular trade. The following guidelines are helpful in engaging more solid trading opportunities:

Trading Opportunities

Intraday Range Trades	
Indicators	Rules
Stochastic	Use hourly charts to determine entry points.
MACD	Use daily charts for range trade confirmation on a longer
RSI	deadline.
Bollinger Bands	Short-dated risk reversals should be near choice.
Options	Reversal oscillators should be at extreme points.
Fibonacci retracement levels	Prices at key resistance points or those that hold key support levels offer stronger trades.

Medium-Term Range Trades	
Indicators	Rules
Stochastic	Use daily charts.
MACD	Position for either of the following:
RSI	Upcoming range trades — seek high volatility environments
Bollinger Bands	where short-term implied volatilities are higher than long-
Options	term. Seek reversion back to the mean environment.
Fibonacci retracement levels	Existing range trades — identify existing ranges using Bollinger bands.
	Seek reversals in oscillators.
	Seek ADX below 25 and falling.
	Seek medium term risk reversals near choice.
	Confirm price action.

Medium-Term Trend Trades

Indicators	Rules
RSI	Use daily charts to locate trends.
Bollinger Bands	Use weekly charts to confirm trends.
ADX	Ensure that characteristics of trending environment are met.
Elliott waves	Buy breakout and retracement on key Fibonacci levels or moving averages.
Parabolic SAR	
Fibonacci	No major resistance levels in front of the trade.
Ichimoku clouds	Seek candlestick pattern for confirmation.
	Seek moving averages on the same side of the trade.
	Enter on a break of significant high or low.
	Ideally, wait for volatilities to contract.
	Seek supporting fundamentals.

Medium-Term Breakout Trades

Indicators	Rules
Bollinger Bands	Use daily charts.
Fibonacci	Seek contraction in short-term volatility sharply below long-term volatility.
Moving averages	
	Use pivot points to distinguish true breaks from false breaks.
	Seek moving averages confluences in support of the trade.

CASE STUDY: AVOID THESE TRADING MISTAKES

Andrew Abraham
Excerpt from Commodity & Forex Trading Mistakes, by Andrew Abraham (www.articlesbase.com/wealth-building-articles/commodity-forex-trading-mistakes-1427052.html)

Andrew Abraham has been investing in commodities and managed futures since 1994 and is a commodity trading adviser and co-manager of a commodity pool. He adheres to the philosophy of trend following.

Trend following stresses a disciplined approach to commodity/futures trading. Successful trend following and commodity futures investing requires patience, discipline, and active risk management. What sets us apart from other commodity trading advisers and commodity pools is that we are not only concerned about the return on investment, but how much risk you will have to tolerate to achieve your goals.

Trading mistakes are common in commodity and forex trading. I became involved with my partners in order to learn from my own mistakes and the mistakes of other commodity traders. In my opinion, after being involved in commodity trading and trend following, the basis of trading mistakes boils down to three issues: fear, greed, ego.

So many issues in trading are against our own human nature. A simple example is that commodity traders risk their hard-earned capital on a trade. Isn't it logical that if you put your hard-earned money in an idea, you would expect it to work and make money? Otherwise, why would you risk hard-earned money? You believe that the trade will make you money, which is why you invested it in the first place, right?

Wrong. Just because you put on the trade does not mean it has to work. Too many traders do not sell and take a quick loss because they think they are right. Guess what? The only thing that is right is to follow your plan with discipline and patience. The real key to successful commodity and forex trading lies in how you think. Emotions, like fear and greed, can destroy your commodity-trading career. I have seen it. I do this every day, except Saturday and Sunday — I live it.

The following are some simple examples of mistakes I have seen commodity traders make:

1. **The commodity trader exits a trade early.** He does not follow his plan … or mechanical trading system. He has a small open trade loss that has not reached his stop loss (limit), and because of fear (maybe ego), he exits prematurely and does not let the trade either get stopped out by the limit or work successfully.

2. **A commodity trader quits trading during a draw down (probably right before a nice rebound).** I have seen investors in commodity trading quit during a draw down and blame the commodity-trading adviser, saying the trend strategy does not work any more, which is a reaction of fear. If they had stayed in with the commodity-trading adviser, shortly thereafter their account would have rebounded, and they would have continued to compound their way to wealth.

3. **I have seen commodity traders take profits and exit before their stop limits have been hit.** They override their plan or mechanical trading system because they are afraid of giving back an open profit. One of the major tenants of trend following is: Let your profits run. These traders miss the big moves because of a combination of fear and maybe greed.

4. **I have seen traders not take a loss when they should have.** Again, they override their plan. Maybe out of ego, they do not want to accept they were wrong and the trade did not work. Even worse, I have seen commodity traders insist they are right and add to their losing position. Actions like this are the seeds of destruction for a commodity trader.

In order to succeed you need to park your emotions and let the market tell you what to do. This is the whole basis of trend following. If you want to succeed in commodity trading, you have choices — you can learn and trade yourself. This takes tremendous work and commitment. I know; I have been there. If you are committed, develop a plan, and follow it with patience and discipline, you at least stand the chance of succeeding over time. An alternative is to allocate the responsibility to an experienced commodity-trading adviser.

You must understand how the commodity trading adviser trades and, probably more important, how he or she thinks about risk and money management. Finding the right commodity-trading adviser is not easy.

Four quick questions can separate the potentially successful commodity-trading advisers from the wannabes:

1. What is their risk per trade?
2. What is their risk per sector?
3. What is their total open trade risk?
4. What is their margin to equity?

Ask these questions and know the answers you are comfortable with. I wish you much success in your commodity-trading career.

Popular Trading Strategies

Each forex trader develops a personal style and adopts one or more trading strategies that suit his or her schedule and interests. There are thousands of possible methods for trading forex. It is impossible for one person to trade the entire forex market; success comes from specializing and becoming thoroughly familiar with a few strategies and currency pairs. Following are descriptions of some well-known trading strategies.

Scalping

Scalping, short-term trading for rapid small profits, is a popular trading strategy that requires extreme discipline and focus. The goal is to make many trades and gain five to 15 pips on each one. The advantage of this strategy is that it is fairly easy to accomplish this goal. The disadvantage is that a single loss can wipe out an entire day's profits.

Professional scalpers make between ten and 100 trades each day. The strategy is to go long or short on a currency pair at the bid or ask price, and then get out of the trade quickly or as soon as the price rises by a few pips. It is essential to use a broker with low spreads and instant execution of trades. Scalpers get out of the market quickly when a trade turns against them to prevent losing trades from absorbing all their profit.

Forex scalpers typically use price charts with intervals of one minute, five minutes, and one hour, and make their profits from relatively minor price fluctuations.

Rules for successful scalping are:

- Identify the overall direction of the market for that day and trade in that direction.

- If you do not feel comfortable with a trade, or the price is not moving as you expected, get out right away.

- Mark trend lines, support and resistance, and pivot points on your hourly and daily price charts.

- Memorize basic technical patterns.

- Keep a record of the previous day's high, low, open, and close.

- If the price moves more than ten pips in your direction, adjust your stop loss order.

- Be aware of any news releases that will affect your currency pair.

Multiple deadline analyses

Profit potential exists for trades that capture and participate in big market movements. One theory suggests 70 percent of a market's moves occur 20 percent of the time. Based on this theory, multiple deadline analyses provide a method for assessing opportunities to buy in an uptrend and sell in a downtrend, rather than trying to pick tops and troughs. Multiple deadline analyses involve using daily charts to identify the overall trend, and then using hourly charts to determine entry levels. For example, if a daily chart shows an uptrend, the trader would take a position in the direction of the trend. The trader would then examine an hourly chart of the Fibonacci retracements drawn from the all-time high of the daily chart to the low of the trend.

Fading the double zeros

One of the lucrative areas of trading involves analyzing the market structure. An understanding of the microstructure and dynamics of the market allows traders to profit from intraday fluctuations. This information is critical to foreign exchange markets because order flow is the primary influence of intraday price actions. Because most traders are not privy to sell-side bank order flow, day traders need to identify and anticipate price zones where large order flows should be triggered, as a way of profiting from short-term market fluctuations. Doing so provides day traders with a technique to get on the same side as the market maker.

Day traders cannot expect to seek out and profit from every support and resistance level. Traders have to be selective and enter at those levels in which reaction is more likely. Trading off double zeros or round numbers is one way of identifying such opportunities. Double zeros are numbers in which the last two digits are zero, such as 168.00 or 1.3400. Currency pairs will bounce off double zero support or resistance levels, despite the underlying trend. The intraday trader will notice that bounces are usually higher and more relevant than bounces off other areas. This type of reaction allows an intraday trader to profit 50 pips while only risking 15 to 20 pips. The psychology of round number levels is even more significant when these levels coincide with other technical levels. The strategy has a higher probability of success when other support and resistance levels converge at the same level.

This strategy requires traders to develop a feel for dealing room and market participant psychology. Large banks have a distinct advantage over other market participants. The banks' order books provide them with direct insight into potential reactions at different price levels. Dealers strategically use this information to put short-term positions on their own accounts. Market participants tend to put conditional orders near the same levels while stop-loss orders are usually placed beyond round numbers. As a result, take-profit orders have a high probability of being placed at the double zero level. Because the forex market operates 24 hours, speculators tend to use stop and limit orders much more than in other markets. Large banks with access to conditional order flow actively seek to exploit the large number of positions in the market. Fading the double zero has the effect of positioning traders for a quick move at the double zero level. This type of trade is most profitable when there are other technical indicators that also confirm the significance of the double zero level. The fading double zeros strategy works best when the move happens under quiet market conditions. The strategy is most successful for commodity currencies, pairs with tighter trading ranges, and crosses. This strategy works for the major currencies (but under quieter market conditions because stops are relatively tight).

Long position rules:

- Seek a currency pair that is trading well below its intraday 20-period SMA on a ten- or 15-minute chart.

- Enter a long position at several pips below this figure, but no more than ten.

- Place initial stop no more than 20 pips below the entry price.

- Double the amount risked when the position is profitable.

- Close half of the position.

- Move the stop on the remaining portion to break even.

- Trail the stop as the price moves favorably.

Short position rules:

- Seek a currency pair that is trading well above its intraday 20-period SMA on a ten- or 15-minute chart.

- Enter a short position at several pips above this figure, but no more than ten.

- Place initial stop no more than 20 pips above the entry price.

- When the position is profitable, double the amount risked.

- Close half of the position.

- Move the stop on the remaining portion to break even (the original purchase price).

- Trail the stop as the price moves favorably.

Waiting for the real deal

The waiting for the real deal strategy involves waiting for market noise to settle down before trading real market price actions. With this strategy, day traders rely more on the microstructure of the market than on the level of demand. Though the forex market operates 24 hours, the extent of trading activity can vary significantly during each trading session. Traditionally, trading activities have been least active during the Asian market hours, meaning some currencies, such as GBP/USD and EUR/USD, trade within tight ranges during this time. A study indicates that as of 2004, the United Kingdom captured 31 percent of the total trading volume, making it the most active trading center. Furthermore, Europe, France, Switzerland, and Germany accounted for 42 percent of the foreign trading volume. The United States was second to the United Kingdom, capturing 19 percent of the volume, particularly important to the London market because this gives traders an opportunity to evaluate events and announcements that occurred in the United States or in the overnight Asian market. The evaluation is particularly critical when the FOMC of the Fed meets and announces monetary policy. Announcements at 2:15 p.m. EST in New York occur after the London market closes.

Another anomaly of market structure that provides opportunities for day traders is during the London and European trading hours, and during the overlap of the U.S. and European trading hours, when the British pound trades most actively against the U.S. dollar. At other times, GBP/USD trades are relatively light, because the majority of trading with this pairing is done through U.K. and European markets. Day traders may capture the initial moves in the London market that usually occur within the first few hours of the trading day. The U.K. and European dealers are the primary market makers for GBP/USD trades, meaning they have insight into the extent of supply and demand for the pair.

Waiting for the real deal strategy starts at the beginning of trading, when interbank dealing desks survey their books and use client data to trigger close stops on both sides of the markets, allowing them to gain pip differential. After the stops are exercised and the books are cleared, the directional move in GBP/USD begins. At this point, traders should check to ensure the rules for this strategy have been met before entering a long or short position. This strategy works best after a major economic release or following the U.S. market opening.

Long position rules:

- Seek GBP/USD pairs to make a new range low, at least 25 pips above the opening price.

- The currency pair should reverse and then penetrate the high.

- Place an entry order to buy ten pips above the average high of the range.

- Place an initial stop at no more than 20 pips from the entry.

- If the position moves lower by twice the amount risked, close half of the position.

- Trail a stop on the remaining position.

Short position rules:

- Seek GBP/USD pairs to make a new range low, at least 25 pips above the opening price.

- The currency pair should reverse and then penetrate the low.

- Place an entry order to sell ten pips below the average low of the range.

- Place an initial stop at no more than 20 pips from the entry.

- If the position moves lower by twice the amount risked, close half of the position.

- Trail a stop on the remaining position.

Inside day breakout play

An inside day occurs when the daily range is contained within the prior day's trading range; the day's highs and lows do not exceed those of the previous day. Breakout traders are able to identify inside days with a basic candlestick chart. There must be two inside days before volatility play can be implemented. The more inside days a trader is able to capture, the higher the probability of a breakout. A breakout is an upside surge in volatility.

This strategy works best with daily charts, though some traders use hourly charts. Daily charts provide the best method of identifying inside days, and daily charts with later deadlines provide the most significant breakout opportunities. Day traders seeking inside days on hourly charts will find that their chances of predicting a solid breakout increase if the contraction precedes London or U.S. market openings. The objective for trades is to predict a valid breakout without being caught in a false breakout move. Traders who use daily charts should seek breakouts before a major economic release for the particular currency pair. Though this works with all currencies pairs, less frequent false breakouts occur in the tighter range currency pairs, such as USD/CAD, EUR/CAD, EUR/GBP, EUR/CHF, and AUD/CAD.

Long position rules:

- Seek multiple inside days. Identify a currency pair where the daily range is contained within the prior day's range for a minimum of two days.

- Buy ten pips above the high of the previous day.

- Place a stop and reverse order for two lots, at least ten pips below the low of the nearest inside day.

- Take the profit when prices double the amount risked or at the level where prices begin to trail the stop.

- To prevent a false breakout, place a stop at least ten pips above the high of the nearest inside day if the stop and reverse order is triggered. Trail the stop to take profits larger than the amount risked.

Short position rules:

- Seek multiple inside days. Identify a currency pair where the daily range is contained within the prior day's range for a minimum of two days.

- Sell ten pips below the low of the previous day.

- Place a stop and reverse order for two lots at least ten pips above the high of the nearest inside day.

- Take the profit when prices double the amount risked or at the level where prices begin to trail the stop.

- To prevent a false breakout, place a stop at least ten pips below the low of the nearest inside day if the stop and reverse order is triggered. Trail the stop to take profits larger than the amount risked.

The fader

The fader strategy is a variation of the waiting for the real deal strategy. This strategy uses daily charts to identify range-bound environments and hourly charts to determine entry points. Traders will eventually find themselves faced with a potential breakout and then position themselves for it, only to have the trade fail and prices revert back to range trading. If prices do break out above significant levels, a continuation of the move is not guaranteed. If the level is very significant, interbank dealers or other traders may try to push prices momentarily beyond the levels to execute stops. There is no rule for determining how much force is needed to carry pricing beyond levels and into a sustainable trend.

Much risk is involved with trading breakouts, and false breakouts may occur more often than actual breakouts. Sometimes prices will test the resistance level once, twice, or three times before breaking out. Contra-trend traders will look to fade breakouts in currency markets. After a breakout occurs, the trend is usually long lasting and strong. As a result, contra-traders' attempts to try to fade every breakout can result in losses. Traders need a method of screening out consolidation patterns for trades that have a higher probability for resulting in false breakouts. The rules provide a basis for such screening.

Long position rules:

- Seek a currency pair with a 14-period ADX less than 35.

- Ideally, the ADX should be following a downward trend indicating a weakening.

- Wait for the market to move below the previous day's low by at least 15 pips.

- Place an initial order to buy 15 pips above the previous day's high.

- Once filled, place the initial stop no more than 30 pips below the entry.

- Take profit when prices double the risk or prices increase by 60 pips.

Short position rules:

- Seek a currency pair with a 14-period ADX less than 35.

- Ideally, the ADX should be following a downward trend indicating a weakening.

- Wait for the market to move above the previous day's high by at least 15 pips.

- Place an initial order to sell 15 pips below the previous day's low.

- Once filled, place the initial stop no more than 30 pips above the entry.

- Take profit when the position moves favorably by 60 pips.

Filtering false breakouts

The rules for this strategy were developed specifically to take advantage of markets with strong trends that make new highs, then fail because of a low, and then reverse again to make new highs. This strategy is successful because it allows traders to enter markets with strong trends after weak players have been pushed out. As a result, only real money players re-enter the market and push the pair up to make major highs.

Trading breakouts can be both profitable and frustrating, because many breakouts have a tendency to fail. One reason for this is the foreign exchange market is more technically driven than other markets. There are many market participants who intentionally break pairs out to un-suspecting traders. In an effort to filter out potential false breakouts, a price action screener is used to identify those breakouts that have the most chance for success.

Long position rules:

- Seek a currency pair with a 20-day high.

- Wait for the pair to reverse to a two-day low over the next three days.

- Buy if the pair trades above the 20-day high within the three days of making the two-day low.

- Place an initial stop a few pips below the original two-day low (see second bullet).

- Take any profit with a trailing stop or take profits when the amount doubles the amount risked.

Short position rules:

- Seek a currency pair with a 20-day low.

- Wait for the pair to reverse to a two-day high over the next three days.

- Sell if the pair trades below the 20-day low within the three days of making the two-day high.

- Place an initial stop a few pips above the original two-day low (see second bullet).

- Take profit with a trailing stop or take profits when the amount doubles the amount risked.

Channel

Drawing a trend line and another line parallel to the trend line creates a channel. Most or all activity of the currency pair falls within the two lines. Channels occur frequently and may be identified by evaluating only a few charts. Currencies rarely spend time in tight trading ranges, and they usually develop strong trends. The channel strategy involves identifying situations in which a price is trading within a narrow channel and then trading in the direction of a breakout from the channel. This strategy is effective when used before the release of some market event, such as an economic news release or just before the opening of a major financial market. There are many instances in which a break of channel is triggered by an economic release. If a channel is formed, a big number is expected to be released and the currency pair is at the top of the channel. The likelihood of a breakout is high. Traders should be poised to buy the breakout rather than fade it.

Long Position Rules:

- Use either an intraday or daily chart.

- Identify a channel with price contained within a narrow range.

- Enter a long position as the price moves above the upper channel line.

- Place a stop just beneath the upper channel line.

- Trail the stop higher as the price move favorably.

Perfect order

The perfect order strategy involves a perfect ordering in moving averages that are sequential. In an upward trend, a perfect order is a situation in which a ten-day SMA is at a higher price level than a 20-day SMA, which is higher than a 50-day SMA, while the corresponding 100-day SMA is below the 50-day SMA, and the 200-day SMA is below the 100-day SMA. In a downward trend, the opposite occurs. The 200-day SMA is at the highest level and the ten-day SMA is at the lowest level. When moving averages are aligned in sequential order, it is a strong indicator of a trending environment. It indicates that the momentum is on the side of trend and serves as multiple levels of support.

Rules:

- Seek a currency pair with moving averages in perfect order.

- Seek an ADX pointing upward, ideally greater than 20.

- Buy five candles after the initial formation of the perfect order, if it still holds.

- For long positions, place an initial stop at the low on the day of the initial crossover.

- For short positions, place an initial stop at the high on the day of the initial crossover.

- Exit the position when the perfect order no longer holds.

TIP: Novice traders should be wary of pitfalls.

An inexperienced trader who immediately makes a profit on his or her first trades may become addicted to making random trades and taking more risk instead of adhering to a solid trading plan. New traders also tend to dwell on losses and think about how they can make back the money they lost on a previous day, a tendency that clouds their judgment and may result in emotional trades that are doomed to fail.

Chapter 9

Passive Investing in Forex

After reading the previous chapters and learning about everything involved in forex trading, you might conclude that you would like to invest in forex, but have neither the time nor the confidence to succeed on your own. If you want exposure to forex in your investment portfolio without being directly involved in trading, you can pay someone else a fee or commission to do the trading for you. Many forex brokers offer managed accounts in which experienced professionals trade in the forex market on your behalf. You can also purchase shares of a forex mutual fund or ETF.

Many forex traders use robots — software applications that automatically search for certain market conditions and place buy and sell orders.

Forex in an Investment Portfolio

Your investment portfolio includes every investment that you purchase with the intention of increasing and protecting your wealth: stocks, bonds, real estate properties, businesses, precious metals, your 401(k) or IRA, annuities, and even life insurance. Financial experts emphasize that the key to increasing your wealth over time is maintaining diversity in your portfolio: investing in assets that behave differently when economic conditions fluctuate so that losses in one area will be compensated for by gains in another. If all of your investments are of the same type, you may flourish under one set of economic conditions but lose everything when those conditions change.

The economic crisis of 2007 to 2009 illustrated how globalization has made the world's markets so interdependent that all asset classes now tend to rise and fall together. A conventional portfolio of stocks and bonds can no longer be considered fully diversified. Stocks rise in value when the economy is strong and businesses are prospering, but the value of currencies rises and falls based on inflation rates and the actions of central banks. The currencies of some countries benefit from the same factors that decrease the value of stock indexes, bonds, or commodities. Fluctuations of currency values are therefore out of sync with the stock markets. For example, from January to December of 2008 the Dow lost 34 percent, while the value of the Japanese yen went up 23 percent against the dollar. Including currencies in your portfolio can provide income and growth when the stock market is in a decline. Currencies also protect against the loss of purchasing power of the dollar due to inflation.

Stocks tend to increase in value over time, and wealth is realized through selling them at a profit and from the dividends paid by some stocks. Currency values rise and fall relative to each other all the time, and profit is realized through active trading. Gains and losses are determined by trading strategy, not by the direction of the market. Conventional financial advisers typically advise against investing in forex because active trading requires a special set of skills that most investors do not have. However, you can add forex to an investment portfolio by setting a managed account with a broker or purchasing a forex mutual fund or ETF. If you have substantial foreign investments or own a business that has interests in foreign countries, investing in currency can also serve as a hedge against losses due to currency fluctuations.

> **TIP: No more than 2 to 5 percent of your
> portfolio should be invested in forex.**
>
> Because of the high risk involved in forex trading, most financial advisers
> recommend that no more than 2 percent of a smaller investment portfolio,
> and 5 percent of a larger portfolio, should be invested in currency trading.

Managed Accounts

In a managed account, investors allow a particular firm or individual
to trade on their behalf. Managed accounts provide investors with an
opportunity to invest in the forex market without direct involvement.
For retail investors in particular, a managed account offers the benefit
of an experienced investment manager's knowledge, experience, and
resources without the investment restrictions that accompany hedge
funds and other types of investment opportunities. Managed accounts
are handled much like mutual funds but with greater risk potential.

You are responsible for selecting an appropriate firm that will manage
your funds well and trade in your best interest. You will be required to
sign a standard account opening document and other documents that
give the manager what is called limited discretion to trade on your behalf and withdraw predetermined fees from the account. These documents do not give the account manager full discretion to control all the
funds in the account. Account managers trade through an FCM or bank
but direct the client to open an account with the chosen firm. Managers
can charge a fee not to exceed 2 percent and can receive no more than
a 20 percent return. Account managers are also required to disclose any
other compensation derived from managed accounts.

In the United States, managed accounts are not required to be registered
with the Securities and Exchange Commission (SEC). If the account
is used strictly in the forex market, there is no requirement for the ac-

count manager to provide disclosure documents, including corporate or personal biographies, audited performance, trading strategies overview, risks, and other information that would assist an investor in making an informed and educated decision. If an investment account is used to trade futures, the account manager is required under CFTC and NFA guidelines to provide potential investors with disclosure documents. CFTC and NFA guidelines also require that the account manager be registered as a Commodity Pool Operator (CPO), commodity-trading adviser (CTA), or a registered investment adviser (RIA) who has educational and filing requirements.

TIP: Watch your expenses.

Managed accounts entail extra management fees. Watch your returns relative to your expenses to confirm that the managed account is a worthwhile investment.

Professional Forex Advisers

Many forex brokers offer the services of professional forex advisers, experienced traders who act as coaches, reviewing your accounts, offering advice and teaching you more complex strategies. Companies like Forex Advisor (**http://forex-advisor.com**) and BK Forex Advisors (**www.bkforexadvisors.com**) provide individualized training by experienced forex traders who analyze your trading style and help you make improvements to your trading strategies.

Forex Robots

One of the main keys to success in forex trading is developing a trading strategy that succeeds more often than it fails and executing it consistently. Experienced forex traders spend days, weeks, and even months testing and adjusting their strategies. A trader sits in front of a computer watching price movements on a set of charts and executes buy and sell orders whenever specific patterns or market conditions occur. It is impossible, however, to monitor the market 24 hours a day, and sometimes fatigue or indecision interferes with a trader's ability to act quickly when an opportunity presents itself. Sometimes a trader has to wait for hours for a particular trading signal to manifest.

Forex robots are software applications programmed to monitor large quantities of market data, and either alert the trader when specific conditions occur, or automatically place buy and sell orders on the trader's behalf. A large number of forex robots are available on the market. Some are sophisticated platforms with ready-made strategies that can handle multiple currencies and large amounts of money; others can be programmed by a trader to execute his or her own personal strategy. Robots eliminate human emotion by trading strictly within pre-programmed parameters and are capable of simultaneously monitoring much more information than any human could. The currency pair most commonly monitored with robots is EUR/USD, but there are also many robots for EUR/GBP, USD/JPY, and AUD/USD.

Expert advisers (EAs) are mechanical trading applications that integrate with the MetaTrader 4 trading platform. They use technical indicators to identify specific market signals, place buy and sell orders and automatically adjust stop-loss and take-profit limits. Each EA is unique and follows specific rules for entering and exiting the market. The trader must link it to a specific chart on the MetaTrader 4 Forex trading platform. An experienced trader might create a portfolio of robots trading different currency pairs, using different strategies over different time frames in order to capture as many opportunities as possible. Large-scale forex investors such as banks and mutual funds use multiple robots as part of their forex trading strategies. A robot should always be monitored because it can fail if the market shifts.

TIP: Be cautious when purchasing a robot.

A robot is only as good as the rules it follows and may not continue to function well when the market shifts. If the rules programmed into a robot are not thoroughly tested, the results could be disastrous. The websites that sell robots make many promises, but you are responsible for verifying that a robot works before entrusting your account to it. Before purchasing an EA, backtest it using historical market data to see whether it produces the promised results. If it passes this test, use a demo account to forward-test it with live-market data. Even a demo account will not provide a completely accurate test. Find out if the robot vendor has tested it in the live forex market. Finally, monitor the robot carefully when you run it on your forex account and make sure it is meeting your expectations.

Forex Hosting and Forex VPS

Earlier in the book, you learned the importance of having a reliable Internet connection and a back-up power supply, as well as an alternative means of communicating with your forex broker if your connection goes down. An open trade could result in large losses if you miss a market signal or are unable to sell when the price starts to drop. This danger is amplified when you are using robots to trade automatically, because you might not be aware of open trades and the robot would be unable to send an order to your broker. A temporary interruption could interfere with a robot and cause it to miss a stop signal and malfunction. If you are using a robot 24 hours a day, your computer must run continuously.

For these reasons, many traders use forex hosting, or a virtual private server (VPS) to run their trading platforms online. For a monthly fee, companies such as Forex Hoster (**www.forexhoster.com**) and Forex VPS (**www.forexvps.com**) offer pre-installed forex platforms that can be linked directly to your broker.

Forex Mutual Funds

The stock market slump of 2007 to 2009 sent startled investors scrambling to find ways to make money during an economic slump, and generated widespread interest in currency mutual funds. A number of open-ended mutual funds (OEFs) exist.

The oldest is the Franklin Templeton Hard Currency (ICHHX), launched in 1989, which "invests in high-quality, short-term money market instruments (and forward currency contracts) denominated in currencies of foreign countries and markets that historically have experienced low inflation rates." (**www.franklintempleton.com/retail/jsp_app/products/fund_facts.jsp?fundNumber=412**).

Merk Mutual Funds (**www.merkfunds.com**) offers a Merk Absolute Return Currency Fund (MABFX), Merk Asian Currency Fund (MEAFX), and the Merk Hard Currency Fund (MERKX), which invests in hard currencies from countries with strong monetary policies. The minimum investment is $1,000.

Rydex SGI (**www.rydex-sgi.com**) offers two open-end funds that use leverage to amplify the rise or fall of the dollar, the Dynamic Strengthening Dollar (RYSBX) and the Dynamic Weakening Dollar Fund (RYWBX). The investment minimum for these funds is $25,000.

ProFunds' (**www.profunds.com**) Rising U.S. Dollar ProFund (RDPIX) and Falling U.S. Dollar ProFund (FDPIX) track daily movements in the U.S. Dollar Index, but do not employ leverage. The minimum investment for individuals is $15,000.

Mutual funds are actively managed by professional fund managers who have expertise and many resources at their disposal. Investing in a mutual fund exposes your portfolio to one or more foreign currencies, without requiring the daily attention you must devote to active forex trading. A mutual fund can also be used as part of a forex trading strategy to hedge losses on the spot forex market. Mutual funds charge management fees that eat into returns.

Currency ETFs

Currency exchange-traded funds (ETFs) buy and hold currencies on behalf of investors, and some of them engage in trading currency futures or leveraged trades. Their shares are bought and sold on the stock exchanges like shares of stock. Simple currency ETFs do not generate income; an investor makes money by selling the shares for more than the purchase price. Fund expenses are covered by the interest earned by the currency, which is deposited in a trustee bank. A share of a currency ETF is valued at 100 times the current exchange rate for that currency. For example, if the current underlying exchange rate for the euro versus the U.S. dollar (EUR/USD) is 1.3715, the CurrencyShares Euro Trust (PSE:FXE) will be priced at priced at $137.15 per share (1.3751 × 100 = $137.51).

The net asset value (NAV) of each share is determined by taking the value of the currency at a specific time each day, adding interest earned, subtracting the fund sponsor's fees, and dividing the result by the number of shares. There may be discrepancies between the NAV and the selling price because of timing differences between when the NAV is calculated and the close of the business day at the New York Stock Exchange, where the ETFs are traded.

You can benefit from currency ETFs by buying and selling them as the market fluctuates, and by using them to hedge against losses from foreign investments due to currency fluctuations. ETFs exist for the U.S. dollar versus the euro, the British pound, the Canadian dollar, Japanese yen, Swiss franc, Australian dollar, Mexican peso, Russian ruble, and Swedish krona. ETF shares, like shares of stock, can be bought on margin, sold short, and sold under options and futures contracts.

TIP: Holding a currency ETF could result in opportunity loss.

You only benefit from a simple currency ETF when you sell shares for more than you paid for them, or when you use them to recoup losses from a foreign investment. Otherwise, the ETF shares are sitting in your portfolio earning no income. If you do not plan to actively trade your currency ETF shares, consider putting that money into another investment that will earn interest.

ETFs have lower expense ratios and greater transparency than mutual funds. Each ETF holds the currency it is named for, and a list of its current holdings can be viewed on the Internet at any time. Mutual fund managers, on the other hand, can change the currency exposure in a mutual fund by buying or selling currencies at their discretion.

Several ETFs, such as ProShares Ultra Euro (ULE) and ProShares Ultra Yen (YCL), use leverage or currency futures to actively generate income from forex trading. You can find information about these funds in the ETF Database on the ETFGuide website (**www.etfguide.com**). Read the prospectus carefully and be sure you fully understand the investment before buying. Most of these ETFs have been in existence for less than two years, so there is little historical information about their performance.

Conclusion

When you step into the exciting world of foreign currency trading, you are joining millions of others actively buying and selling 24 hours a day. Though forex trading is often touted as an easy way to "get rich quick," you have seen from this book that it requires time, patience, self-discipline, and skills, all of which can only be acquired with time and experience. If you have the right qualities, forex trading can be both thrilling and profitable.

The explosion of the Internet over the past two decades has created unprecedented opportunities to trade in a market that was historically open only to large banks and financial institutions. However, electronic methods of currency trading are still in their technological infancy. Controls and safeguards, including those usually imposed by governmental bodies, have not yet been implemented to protect investors from unforeseen loss or exploitation by other more-experienced market participants. Large banks and financial institutions, though they do not completely dominate the forex market, are still poised to manipulate the market and market pricing. Inexperienced market participants must be prepared to begin slowly and carefully, and to protect themselves by doing research, limiting risk and exercising emotional self-control in the face of temptation.

Thousands of forex dealers and brokers, forums, blogs, financial journals and investment sites offer information, education, tutorials, and advice for forex traders. Learn to distinguish between marketing hype and genuinely helpful information. Follow the good suggestions offered by so many fellow traders: Do not invest more than you can afford to lose, get out of losing situations quickly, and use leverage carefully. Keep your trading simple, and master one strategy before adding another one to your arsenal. Use the vast library of resources in print and on the Internet to educate yourself, and become an expert in your field.

Forex trading is not just a way of generating wealth. By studying the markets and learning about the economic and psychological factors that influence price movements, you will broaden your mind and learn to think deeply about the issues that affect the world financially. You are embarking on an adventure that will continue to open new horizons for as long as you pursue it.

This book is intended as an introduction to forex. All the topics mentioned here can be studied in much greater depth. Do not leave your questions unanswered. Instead, keep asking until you are confident that you understand completely.

Happy trading!

Appendix A

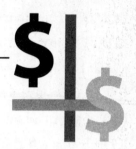

Acronyms Found in This Book

ADV: Average Daily Volume

ADX: Average Directional Index

ASEAN: Association of Southeast Asian Nations

ASIC: Australian Securities and Investment Commission

BEA: U.S. Bureau of Economic Analysis

BIS: Bank for International Settlements

BOC: Bank of Canada

BOE: Bank of England

BOJ: Bank of Japan

BoP: Balance of Payments

CESR: Committee of European Securities Regulators

CLS: Continuous Link Settlement

CME: Chicago Mercantile Exchange

CFTC: Commodity Futures Trading Commission

CPI: Consumer Price Index

CPO: Commodity Pool Operator

CTA: Commodity Trading Adviser

DCIO: Division of Clearing and Intermediary Oversight

DCM: Designated Contract Market

EA: Expert Adviser

EBS: Electronic Broking System

ECB: European Central Bank

ECI: U.S. Employment Cost Index

ECN: Electronic Communication Network

EMU: Economic and Monetary Union

ESCB: European System of Central Banks

EST: Eastern Standard Time

ETF: Exchange Traded Fund

EU: European Union

FCM: Futures Commission Merchant

Fed: U.S. Federal Reserve

FINRA: Financial Industry Regulatory Agency

FLO: Federal Labor Office of Germany

FOMC: Federal Open Market Committee

FRB: Federal Reserve Board

FSA: Financial Services Authority of the United Kingdom

FX: Foreign Exchange

FXCM: Forex Capital Markers

G8: A group of eight of the world's richest economies

G10: Group of Ten

GDP: Gross Domestic Product

GFD: "Good For the Day"

GTC: "Good 'Til Canceled"

GILTS: Gilt Edged Securities

HICP: Harmonized Index of Consumer Prices

HSBC: Hong Kong and Shanghai Banking Corporation

IB: Introductory Broker

IP: Industrial Production

IDAC: Investment Dealers Association of Canada

IFO: Institut für Wirtschaftsforschung an der Universität München

IMM: International Monetary Market

IOSCO: International Organization of Securities Commissions

IP: Industrial Production

IRD: Interest Rate Differential

IIROC: Investment Industry Regulatory Organization of Canada

ISM: Institute for Supply Management

KoF: Konjunkturforschungsstelle der ETH (Zurich, Switzerland)

LIBOR: London Interbank Offered Rates

LVTS: Canadian Large Value Transfer System

M3: Money3

M&A: Merger and acquisition

MACD: Moving Average Convergence/Divergence

MAP: Materially Affiliated Person

MOF: Ministry of Finance (Japan)

MPC: Monetary Policy Committee (UK)

MUIP: Monetary Union Index of Consumer Prices

NASDAQ: National Association of Securities Dealers Automatic Quotation System

NFA: National Futures Association

NSA: Non-Seasonally Adjusted

NYBT: New York Board of Trade

NYSE: New York Stock Exchange

NZS: New Zealand Superannuation

OCR: Official Cash Rate

OEF: Open Ended Fund

OHLC: Open/High/Low/Close

OTC: Over The Counter

PIP: Price Interest Point

P/L: Profit and Loss

PMI: Purchasing Managers Index

PPI: Producer Price Index

PPP: Purchasing Power Parity

PTA: Policy Target Agreement

RBA: Reserve Bank of Australia

RBNZ: Reserve Bank of New Zealand

RIA: Registered Investment Adviser

RMM: Retail Market Maker

RPI: Retail Price Index

RPI-X: Retail Price Index Excluding Mortgage Payments

RSI: Relative Strength Index

RSI: Retail Sales Index

SA: Seasonally Adjusted

SAR: Stop and Reverse

SEC: Securities and Exchange Commission

SFBC: Swiss Federal Banking Commission

SFC: Securities and Futures Commission of Hong Kong

SMA: Simple Moving Average

SNB: Swiss National Bank

STP: Straight-Through Processing

TIC: Treasury International Capital Flow

USDIX: U.S. Dollar Index

VPS: Virtual Private Server

WYC/WYG: "What you click is what you get"

Appendix B

Forex Glossary

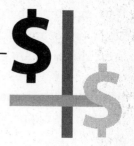

A

Ad hoc: Latin "for this purpose;" a situation that applies only to a specific set of circumstances.

American style option: An option contract that can be exercised at any time before the expiry date.

American terms: A quote in which the value of another currency is given in U.S. dollars.

Anti-dollar: The euro.

Arbitrage: The purchase or sale of a currency while simultaneously taking the opposite position in a related market in order to profit from price differentials.

Ask price: The price for which the market is prepared to sell a specific currency pair.

Ask spread (bid spread): The difference between the ask price and the bid price of a currency pair.

Average Directional Index (ADX): Developed by J. Welles Wilder, ADX measures the strength of market trends on a scale of 0 to 100.

B

Balance of trade: A measure of the net difference between a nation's imports and exports, as measured over time.

Bank rate: The interest rate on overnight borrowing and lending among commercial banks.

Base currency: The currency being bought in a trade.

Basis point: One hundredth of one percent, used to express bond yields and interest rates.

Bear market: A period during which prices are falling and market participants are pessimistic.

Bid/ask spread: The difference between the bid price and the ask price.

Bid price: The price for which the market is prepared to buy a specific currency pair.

Big figure quote: A quote that includes the first few digits of the exchange rate for a currency pair.

Big Mac Index: A comparison of the price of a McDonald's Big Mac sandwich in different countries, used to determine if a currency is undervalued or overvalued.

Bollinger band: A pair of trading bands on a chart representing the predictable upper and lower trading range for a particular market price.

Bookmakers: Websites that facilitate the placing of bets on foreign currency moves.

Breakout: An upside surge in volatility.

Bucket shops: Fraudulent Forex platforms that offer futures and forwards trades in order to swindle investors.

Bull market: A prolonged period during which prices continue to rise.

C

Call option: The right to buy a currency under an option contract.

Candlestick chart: A chart in which market prices are represented by vertical bars with shadows.

Capacity utilization: Industrial production (IP), a measure of industrial capacity and available industrial resources.

Carry: The return on an investment (if positive) or the cost of holding it (if negative).

Carry trade: A trade in which a currency with a lower interest rate is borrowed and sold to purchase an asset bearing a higher interest rate.

Channel: The area between two or more trend lines drawn through.

Channel pattern: A pattern in which trend lines drawn through peaks and troughs are generally flat.

Click-and-deal trading: A trading system in which traders can see live price information and instantly select from trades.

Closing price: The price of a currency pair at the time when the international forex market, or an individual forex market, closes.

Consolidation: A period during which a currency price fluctuates up and down within certain parameters without making a definite move up or down.

Consumer price index (CPI): An index of the cost of a basket of consumer goods and services.

Correlation: The extent to which two investments move up and down in the market together.

Counterparty: The other party in a currency trade.

Cross currency pairs: Two currencies that are traded for each other.

Cross rate: The exchange rate for a currency pair that does not include U.S. dollars or the euro.

Currency board: Another term for the peg system.

Currency pair: The two currencies involved in a trade.

D

Day trader: A short-term trader who takes quick profits and closes out all trades at the end of each day.

Dealer: A firm that acts as the counterparty in foreign exchange trades.

Devaluation: A drop in the value of a currency relative to the value of another currency.

Differentials: The difference between the average foreign interest rate and the U.S. interest rate.

Direct terms: A quote in which the value of another currency is given in U.S. dollars.

Dirty float: A system in which prices are driven both by market demands and by government intervention.

Discount: A forward contract sold at a lower price than its spot value.

Durable goods: Goods that last more than three years.

Durable services: Services that last for more than three years.

Duration: The length of time that a trader requires a broker to keep an un-triggered limit order active.

E

Economic indicators: Indices and statistical measurements that are used to gauge the health of the economy.

Electronic communication network (ECN): An Internet or other electronic data exchange that allows the immediate transaction of currency trades.

Employment Cost Index (ECI): An estimated measure of the number of jobs in more than 500 industries in the United States.

Entry point: The price in a trading system at which a trader buys a currency pair.

Expert adviser: A software application that monitors market activity and identifies trading opportunities through technical analysis.

Euribor rate: A three-month fixed interest rate offered from one large bank to another on euro interbank terms of deposit.

Euro: The common currency of the Economic and Monetary Union.

Euro system: The twelve nations that use the euro plus Great Britain, Sweden, and Denmark.

Eurodollars: U.S. dollars deposited at foreign banks and other foreign financial institutions.

Economic and Monetary Union (EMU): Twelve European nations that share the euro as their currency.

European style option: An option that can only be exercised on or near its expiry date.

European terms: A quote in which the U.S. dollar is the base currency.

Executable streaming price feed: Another name for click-and-deal trading.

Exit point: The price in a trading system at which a trader sells a currency pair.

Exotics: Currencies of lesser-known countries.

Expiry: The length of time that a trader requires a broker to keep an un-triggered limit order active.

F

Fibonacci retracements: Measurements of the percentage by which individual prices reverse from an overall trend.

Fixed income assets: Investments that offer a specified return such as interest or dividends.

Flags and pennants pattern: A continuation pattern in which trend lines drawn through peaks parallel those drawn through troughs, representing a period of indecision.

Forex: Foreign exchange.

Forward trade: A trade in which the date of delivery for a commodity is established for some time in the future.

Free float: A system in which prices are determined by supply and demand, without intervention.

Fresh news: Any unforeseen event that cannot possibly be factored into current pricing.

Fundamentals: The underlying factors that influence economic or business patterns.

Futures commission merchant (FCM): A broker or brokerage that receives and executes orders on behalf of clients and extends credit for margin transactions.

Futures trade: A contract binding a buyer and seller in a trade of currency for a predetermined price at some predetermined time in the future.

G

Gearing: Another term for leverage, the ability to control large sums with a small investment.

G-8: The Group of Eight; eight economic powers: Canada, France, Germany, Italy, Japan, Russia, the United Kingdom, and the United States.

G10: The Group of Ten; eleven industrial countries (Belgium, Canada, France, Germany, Italy, Japan, the Netherlands, Sweden, Switzerland, the United Kingdom, and the United States) that consult and co-operate on economic, monetary, and financial matters.

Gilt Edged Securities (Gilts): Bonds issued by the UK government that offer the investor a fixed interested rate for a predetermined, set time.

Gross domestic product (GDP): The total market value of all goods and services produced by both domestic and foreign companies within a nation's borders.

H

Head and shoulders pattern: A price fluctuation pattern in which a large fluctuation is preceded and followed by smaller fluctuations.

Hedger: A financial entity or investor who uses forex to hedge against losses caused by fluctuations in exchange rates.

Hedging: Minimizing risk exposure by entering both sides of a currency trade.

Home: The level of trading on which a trader bases trading strategy.

Housing starts: The number of new homes that begin construction during a specified period.

Hub and spoke: A network that allows traders to view multiple bids and choose their own counterparties.

I

Ichimoku clouds: A technical indicator that uses five lines to gauge a trend's momentum along with future areas of support and resistance.

Indirect terms: A quote in which the US dollar is the base currency.

Industrial production (IP): A measure of a nation's industrial capacity and available industrial resources.

Inflation: The upward price movement of goods and services within an economy.

Inside day: A day on which the high and low prices are within the previous day's trading range.

Institutional Forex: An Intranet-based trading system of EBS, a consortium of nearly 200 banks that account for more than 50 percent of Forex bank trades.

Interbank market: A loose network of currency trading among banks and financial institutions.

Interest rate differential: The interest charged for a rollover.

Intervention: The attempt by a government to actively influence the price of its currency.

L

Lagging indicators: Elements of economics that change after an economy has already begun to follow a particular trend or pattern.

Law of one price: The principle that, excluding transaction costs, competitive markets will equalize the price of identical goods in two nations when prices are expressed in the same currency.

Leading indicators: Economic elements that change before an economy begins to follows a particular trend or pattern.

Liquidity: The ease with which a currency can be bought or sold.

Limit order: A market order that sets a price limit for selling or buying.

Limited discretion: The amount of authority given to the manager of a fund.

Long position: The position of having purchased a currency in the expectation that the price will rise.

Lot: A standardized trading unit of $1,000 leveraged 100:1.

M

M3: A measure of the amount of money that is commercially available within an economic system.

Major currencies: The seven currencies that experience the highest trading volume: USD, EUR, JPY, GBP, CHF, CAD, and AUD.

Margin: Investment funds loaned to a trader by a broker to increase capital investment by a specified percentage.

Margin account: An account used to hold money as a security deposit for trades.

Market maker(s): The person or persons in a Forex firm who decide pricing for currency trades.

Market order: An order to buy and sell currency at the current market price.

Mini lot: One tenth of a standard lot; a standardized trading unit of $100 also leveraged 100:1.

Minor currencies: All currencies other than the seven major currencies.

Moving average: An average over a specified period of time that is recalculated at regular time intervals.

Moving average convergence/divergence (MACD): An oscillator calculated by subtracting a 12-day exponential moving average value from a 26-day exponential moving average value.

N

News straddle: A trading strategy in which trades with exit and stop orders are placed on both sides of an associated currency pair to take advantage of temporary volatility while the market responds to new information about an unfolding event.

O

One-click dealing: Click-and-deal trading.

Opening price: The initial price at which a currency pair trades when the international forex market, or an individual forex market, opens.

Option: A contract that gives the option to buy or sell a currency for a specified price by a specified date.

Option barrier limit: An option that is exercised when the market price reaches a specified limit.

Order cancels others: A combination of two limit orders, two stop orders, or a limit order and a stop order in which the execution of one order automatically cancels the other.

Oscillator: A tool used for technical analysis in which a value fluctuates between two parameters.

Overnight rate: The interest rate on overnight borrowing and lending among commercial banks.

P

Peg system: System in which domestic currency rates are fixed to a single foreign currency or group of currencies.

Pip: Price interest point; the smallest unit of price expressed for any traded currency.

Pip currency: The second currency in a currency pair.

Platform: A software application used by a retail forex broker to facilitate trades.

Point: Price interest point; also referred to as a "pip."

Position trader: A long-term trader who holds trades overnight or for longer periods of time.

Premium: A forward contract sold at a higher price than its spot value.

Price movement: A measure of the slope of the trend from some defined beginning to end point.

Principal: The amount of currency that can be bought under an option.

Producer price index (PPI): An index that measures the changes in wholesale prices of goods over time.

Purchasing power parity (PPP): The theory that the exchange rates between two currencies are in equilibrium when the purchasing power of the currency is the same in each nation.

Put option: The right to sell a currency under an option contract.

Pyramiding: The process of adding to a favorable open position by initiating new orders in the same currency pair and in the same position.

Q

Quote currency: The currency being sold in a trade.

R

Repo rate: The interest rate used in U.K. monetary policy to meet targets for inflation set by the Treasury.

Request for quote trading: A system in which the trader requests a quote for a specific currency and trade size.

Resistance: A price point above the current market price, where selling reverses an upward trend.

Revaluate: To increase the value of a currency relative to another nation's currency.

Risk reversal: The putting of both a call and put option on the same currency.

Risk/reward ratio: A measure that compares the amount of risk to the amount of reward for a currency trade.

Rollover: The process of rolling an open trade settlement forward to another date.

Round-turn trade: The buy of trade and an offsetting sell or a sell of trade and an offsetting buy of trade of the same size in the same currency pair.

Relative strength index (RSI): An indicator that measures whether the market is overbought or oversold on a scale of 0 to 100.

Round-turn commission: A commission charged on both the purchase and sale of a futures contract.

S

Safe haven commodity: A commodity that is regarded as a very stable investment.

Scalping: The trading of currency pairs with low spreads at short intervals of a few seconds or minutes, in an attempt to gain 3 to 5 pips per trade.

Short position: The position of having sold a currency with the expectation that the price will fall.

Speculator: An investor who makes money based on price increases.

Spot: The price at which you can buy or sell a currency at the present moment.

Spot trade: The immediate purchase or sale of a currency pair at the current quoted price.

Stochastic model: A model based on the premise that as prices increase or decrease, closing prices tend to approximate more and more closely to the high or low prices for a given period.

Stop and Reverse (SAR): An indicator that shows dots, or points, on a price chart wherever there are potential reversals in price movement.

Stop-loss order differential: The number of pips below the entry price that a stop-limit order is placed in a long trade and vice versa in a short trade.

Stop order: An order that occurs when a predetermined price automatically triggers a trade.

Straight-through processing: A trading system in which no time elapses between when a trade is placed and when it is accepted.

Streaming: A data feed that is constantly updated.

Strike price: The price at which an option can be exercised.

Support: A price point below the current market price at which buying reverses a downward trend.

Swap: An arrangement in which one currency is exchanged for another under the provision that it will be returned when certain conditions are achieved.

Symmetrical triangle pattern: A continuation pattern where market data may be encapsulated in a right triangle.

T

Take-profit order differential: The number of pips above the entry price that a take-profit order is placed in a long trade and vice versa in a short trade.

Tick: The smallest interval of time that occurs with a trade.

Trade deficit: An economic condition in which the value of a nation's imports exceeds the value of its exports.

Trading environment: The market circumstances in which a trader operates, usually referring to a trending or ranging market.

Tranche: A loan provided by the IMF to assist a country suffering economic hardship.

Transaction cost: The cost for a round-turn trade.

Trend lines: Lines on a historical price chart that indicate the direction and magnitude of a price trend.

Trend line channel: The area between two trend lines, one drawn through the peaks and the other through the troughs of a price chart.

Trend slope: The slope of a trend from some defined beginning to end point.

Triangular arbitrage: A Forex trading strategy that uses three currencies.

Triangular pattern: A pattern in which prices fluctuate evenly, but the fluctuation becomes progressively smaller before a breakout.

V

Volatility: A measure of how much a price changes over time.

W

Wedge pattern: A continuation pattern in which trend lines drawn through the peaks and troughs intersect to form an angle pointing either upward or downward.

Appendix C

International Currencies

Country	Currency Code	Currency	Country Code
United Arab Emirates	AED	UAE Dirham	AE
Afghanistan	AFA	Afghani	AF
Albania	ALL	Lek	AL
Armenia	AMD	Dram (Russian Ruble [RUR] was formerly in use)	AM
Netherlands Antilles	ANG	Netherlands Antilles Guilder (Florin)	AN
Angola	AON (replacement for AOK)	New Kwanza (replacement for Kwanza)	AO
Argentina	ARA, ARS (replacement for ARP)	Austral and Argentinian Nuevo Peso (replacement for the Peso)	AR
Australia	AUD	Australian Dollar	AU
Christmas Island	AUD	Australian Dollar	CX
Cocos (Keeling) Islands	AUD	Australian Dollar	CC
Heard and McDonald Islands	AUD	Australian Dollar	HM
Kiribati	AUD	Australian Dollar	KI
Nauru	AUD	Australian Dollar	NR
Norfolk Island	AUD	Australian Dollar	NF
Tuvalu	AUD	Australian Dollar	TV
Aruba	AWG	Aruban Florin	AW

Azerbaijan	AZM	Azerbaijani Manat (Russian Ruble [RUR] was formerly in use)	AZ
Bosnia & Herzegovina	BAM	Convertible Mark	BA
Barbados	BBD	Barbados Dollar	BB
Bangladesh	BDT	Taka	BD
Bulgaria	BGL	Bulgarian Lev	BG
Bahrain	BHD	Bahraini Dinar	BH
Burundi	BIF	Burundi Franc	BI
Bermuda	BMD	Bermudian Dollar	BM
Brunei Darussalam	BND	Brunei Dollar	BN
Bolivia	BOB, BOP	Bolivian Boliviano	BO
Brazil	BRL	Cruzeiro Real	BR
Bahamas	BSD	Bahamian Dollar	BS
Bhutan	BTN (also INR)	Ngultrum (Indian Rupee also circulates)	BT
Botswana	BWP	Pula	BW
Belarus (formerly known as Byelorussia)	BYR	Belarussian Ruble (Russian Ruble [RUR] was formerly in use)	BY
Belize	BZD	Belize Dollar	BZ
Canada	CAD	Canadian Dollar	CA
Congo, Democratic Republic of the (formerly Zaïre)	CDZ (formerly ZRZ)	New Zaïre	CD (formerly ZR)
Liechtenstein	CHF	Swiss Franc	LI
Switzerland	CHF	Swiss Franc	CH
Chili	CLP	Chilean Peso	CL
China	CNY	Yuan Renminbi	CN
Colombia	COP	Colombian Peso	CO
Costa Rica	CRC	Costa Rican Colón	CR
Serbia and Montenegro (formerly in Yugoslavia)	CSD, EUR	Serbian Dinar (Serbia), Euro (Montenegro), Euro (Kosovo & Metohia)	CS

Cuba	CUP	Cuban Peso	CU
Cape Verde	CVE	Escudo Caboverdiano	CV
Cyprus	CVP	Cypriot Pound	CY
Czech Republic	CZK	Czech Koruna	CZ
Djibouti	DJF	Djibouti Franc	DJ
Denmark	DKK	Danish Krone	DK
Faroe Islands	DKK	Danish Krone	FO
Greenland	DKK	Danish Krone	GL
Dominican Republic	DOP	Dominican Republic Peso	DO
Algeria	DZD	Algerian Dinar	DZ
Estonia	EEK	Kroon	EE
Egypt	EGP	Egyptian Pound	EG
Eritrea	ERN, ETB	Eritrean Nakfa, Ethiopian Birr	ER
Ethiopia	ETB	Birr	ET
Andorra	EUR	Euro	AD
Austria	EUR	Euro	AT
Belgium	EUR	Euro	BE
Finland	EUR	Euro	FI
France	EUR	Euro	FR
France, Metropolitan	EUR	Euro	FX
French Guiana	EUR	Euro	GF
French Southern and Antarctic Territories	EUR	Euro	TF
Germany (West and East)	EUR	Euro	DE (formerly DE for West and DD for East)
Greece	EUR	Euro	GR
Guadeloupe	EUR	Euro	GP
Holy See (Vatican City State)	EUR	Euro	VA

Ireland	EUR	Euro	IE
Italy	EUR	Euro	IT
Luxembourg	EUR	Euro	LU
Martinique	EUR	Euro	MQ
Mayotte	EUR	Euro	YT
Monaco	EUR	Euro	MC
Netherlands	EUR	Euro	NL
Portugal	EUR	Euro	PT
Réunion	EUR	Euro	RE
San Marino	EUR	Euro	SM
Spain	EUR	Euro	ES
St Pierre and Miquelon	EUR	Euro	PM
European Community	EUR (formerly XEU)	Euro (formerly known as the ECU)	??
Fiji Islands	FJD	Fiji Dollar	FJ
Falkland Islands (Malvinas)	FKP	Falkland Pound	FK
South Georgia and the South Sandwich Islands	GBP	Pound Sterling	GS
United Kingdom	GBP (sometimes incorrectly seen as UKP)	Pound Sterling	GB
British Indian Ocean Territory	GBP, SCR	Pound Sterling (United Kingdom Pound), Seychelles Rupee	IO
Georgia	GEL	Lari (Russian Ruble [RUR] was formerly in use)	GE
Ghana	GHC	Cedi	GH
Gibraltar	GIP	Gibraltar Pound	GI
Gambia	GMD	Dalasi	GM
Guinea	GNS	Guinea Syli (also known as Guinea Franc)	GN
Guatemala	GTQ	Quetzal	GT
Guinea-Bissau	GWP, XAF	Guinea-Bissau Peso and Franc de la Communauté Financière Africaine	GW

Guyana	GYD	Guyana Dollar	GY
Hong Kong	HKD	Hong Kong Dollar	HK
Honduras	HNL	Lempira	HN
Haiti	HTG	Gourde	HT
Hungary	HUF	Forint	HU
Indonesia	IDR	Rupiah	ID
Israel	ILS	Israeli New Shekel	IL
India	INR	Indian Rupee	IN
Iraq	IQD	Iraqi Dinar	IQ
Iran, Islamic Republic of	IRR	Iranian Rial	IR
Iceland	ISK	Icelandic Króna	IS
Jamaica	JMD	Jamaican Dollar	JM
Jordan	JOD	Jordanian Dinar	JO
Japan	JPY	Yen	JP
Kenya	KES	Kenyan Shilling	KE
Kyrgyzstan	KGS	Kyrgyzstani Som	KG
Cambodia (formerly Kampuchea)	KHR	Riel	KH
Comoros	KMF	Comorian Franc	KM
Korea, Democratic People's Republic of (North Korea)	KPW	North Korean Won	KP
Korea, Republic of (South Korea)	KRW	South Korean Won	KR
Kuwait	KWD	Kuwaiti Dinar	KW
Cayman Islands	KYD	Cayman Islands Dollar	KY
Kazakhstan	KZT	Tenge (Russian Ruble [RUR] was formerly in use)	KZ
Lao People's Democratic Republic (formerly Laos)	LAK	Kip	LA
Lebanon	LBP	Lebanese Pound	LB

Sri Lanka	LKR	Sri Lankan Rupee	LK
Liberia	LRD	Liberian Dollar	LR
Lesotho	LSL, LSM, ZAR	Loti, Maloti and South African Rand	LS
Lithuania	LTL	Litas	LT
Latvia	LVL	Lats	LV
Libyan Arab Jamahiriya	LYD	Libyan Dinar	LY
Morocco	MAD	Moroccan Dirham	MA
Western Sahara	MAD, MRO	Moroccan Dirham and Mauritanian Ouguiya	EH
Moldova, Republic of	MDL	Moldovian Leu	MD
Madagascar	MGF	Madagascar (Malagasi) Franc	MG
Macedonia, the Former Yugoslav Republic of	MKD	Macedonian Denar	MK
Myanmar (formerly Burma)	MMK (formerly BUK)	Kyat	MM (formerly BU)
Mongolia	MNT	Tugrik	MN
Macao (also spelled Macau)	MOP	Pataca	MO
Mauritania	MRO	Ouguiya	MR
Malta	MTL (MTP formerly in use)	Maltese Lira (Maltese Pound formerly in use)	MT
Mauritius	MUR	Mauritius Rupee	MU
Maldives	MVR	Rufiyaa	MV
Malawi	MWK	Malawian Kwacha	MW
Mexico	MXN (replacement for MXP)	Mexican New Peso (replacement for Mexican Peso)	MX
Malaysia	MYR	Ringgit (Malaysian Dollar)	MY
Mozambique	MZM	Metical	MZ
Namibia	NAD, ZAR	Namibian Dollar and South African Rand	NA
Nigeria	NGN	Naira	NG
Nicaragua	NIO	Córdoba Oro	NI
Norway	NOK	Norwegian Krone	NO

Svalbard and Jan Mayen Islands	NOK	Norwegian Krone	SJ
Nepal	NPR	Nepalese Rupee	NP
Cook Islands	NZD	New Zealand Dollar	CK
New Zealand	NZD	New Zealand Dollar	NZ
Niue	NZD	New Zealand Dollar	NU
Pitcairn Island	NZD	New Zealand Dollar	PN
Tokelau	NZD	New Zealand Dollar	TK
Oman	OMR	Rial Omani	OM
Panama	PAB, USD	Balboa and US Dollar	PA
Peru	PEI, PEN (PEN replaced PES)	Nuevo Sol (New Sol replaced Sol)	PE
Papua New Guinea	PGK	Kina	PG
Philippines	PHP	Philippines Peso	PH
Pakistan	PKR	Pakistani Rupee	PK
Poland	PLN (replacement for PLZ)	New Zloty (replacement for Zloty)	PL
Paraguay	PYG	Guarani	PY
Qatar	QAR	Qatari Riyal	QA
Romania	ROL	Romanian Leu	RO
Serbia	RSD	Dinar	CS
Russian Federation	RUB (formerly RUR)	Russian Federation Ruble	RU
Rwanda	RWF	Rwanda Franc	RW
Saudi Arabia	SAR	Saudi Riyal	SA
Solomon Islands	SBD	Solomon Islands Dollar	SB
Seychelles	SCR	Seychelles Rupee	SC
Sudan	SDP, SDD	Sudanese Pound and Sudanese Dinar	SD
Sweden	SEK	Swedish Krona	SE
Singapore	SGD	Singapore Dollar	SG
St Helena	SHP	St. Helenian Pound	SH
Slovenia	EUR	Euro	SI
Slovakia (Slovak Republic)	SKK	Slovak Koruna	SK

Sierra Leone	SLL	Leone	SL
Somalia	SOS	Somali Shilling	SO
Suriname	SRG	Surinam Guilder (also known as Florin)	SR
São Tomé and Príncipe	STD	Dobra	ST
El Salvador	SVC	El Salvadorian Colón	SV
Syrian Arab Republic	SYP	Syrian Pound	SY
Swaziland	SZL	Lilangeni	SZ
Thailand	THB	Baht	TH
Tajikistan	TJR	Tajik Ruble (Russian Ruble [RUR] was formerly in use)	TJ
Turkmenistan	TMM	Turkmenistan Manat	TM
Tunisia	TND	Tunisian Dinar	TN
Tonga	TOP	Pa'anga	TO
East Timor	TPE	Timorian Escudo, American and Australian Dollar	TP
Turkey	TRL	New Turkish Lira	TR
Trinidad and Tobago	TTD	Trinidad and Tobago Dollar	TT
Taiwan	TWD	New Taiwan Dollar	TW
Tanzania, United Republic of	TZS	Tanzanian Shilling	TZ
Ukraine	UAH, UAK, UAG	Hryvnia	UA
Uganda	UGS	Ugandan Shilling	UG
American Samoa	USD	US Dollar	AS
Guam	USD	US Dollar	GU
Marshall Islands	USD	US Dollar	MH
Micronesia, Federated States of	USD	US Dollar	FM
Northern Mariana Islands	USD	US Dollar	MP
Palau	USD	US Dollar	PW
Puerto Rico	USD	US Dollar	PR

Turks and Caicos Islands	USD	US Dollar	TC
United States Minor Outlying Islands	USD	US Dollar	UM
United States of America	USD	US Dollar	US
Virgin Islands (US)	USD	US Dollar	VI
Virgin Islands (British)	USD (also GBP, XCD)	US Dollar (Pound Sterling and East Caribbean Dollar also circulate)	VG
Ecuador	USD (ECS)	US Dollar (superseded Sucre in 2000)	EC
Uruguay	UYU (replacement for UYP)	Uruguayan Peso	UY
Uzbekistan	UZS	Uzbekistani Som (Russian Ruble [RUR] was formerly in use)	UZ
Venezuela	VEB	Bolivar	VE
Viet Nam	VND	Dông	VN
Vanuatu	VUV	Vatu	VU
Samoa	WST	Tala	WS
Benin	XAF	Communauté Financière Africaine Franc	BJ
Burkina Faso	XAF	Communauté Financière Africaine Franc	BF
Cameroon	XAF	CFA Central African Franc	CM
Central African Republic	XAF	Communauté Financière Africaine Franc	CF
Chad	XAF	Communauté Financière Africaine Franc	TD
Congo-Brazza-ville	XAF	Communauté Financière Africaine Franc	CG
Congo-Kin-shasa	CDF	Congolese Franc	CG
Gabon	XAF	Communauté Financière Africaine Franc	GA
Ivory Coast (Côte d'Ivoire)	XAF	Communauté Financière Africaine Franc	CI
Togo	XOF	Communauté Financière Africaine Franc	TG

Equatorial Guinea	XAF, GQE	Franc de la Communauté Financière Africaine and Ekwele	GQ
Mali	XOF	Franc de la Communauté Financière Africaine and Malian Franc	ML
Anguilla	XCD	East Caribbean Dollar	AI
Antigua and Barbuda	XCD	East Caribbean Dollar	AG
Dominica	XCD	East Caribbean Dollar	DM
Grenada	XCD	East Caribbean Dollar	GD
Montserrat	XCD	East Caribbean Dollar	MS
Saint Kitts (Christopher) and Nevis	XCD	East Caribbean Dollar	KN
Saint Lucia	XCD	East Caribbean Dollar	LC
Saint Vincent and the Grenadines	XCD	East Caribbean Dollar	VC
Niger	XOF	West African Franc and Franc de la Communauté Financière Africaine	NE
Senegal	XOF	West African Franc and Franc de la Communauté Financière Africaine	SN
French Polynesia	XPF	Franc des Comptoirs Français du Pacifique	PF
New Caledonia	XPF	Franc des Comptoirs Français du Pacifique	NC
Wallis and Futuna Islands	XPF	Franc des Comptoirs Français du Pacifique	WF
Yemen (unified North and South)	YER	Riyal (Dinar was used in South Yemen)	YE (formerly YE for North Yemen and YD for South Yemen)
South Africa	ZAR	Rand	ZA
Zambia	ZMK	Zambian Kwacha	ZM
Zimbabwe	ZWD	Zimbabwe Dollar	ZW

Appendix D

U.S. Forex Brokers

This listing of U.S. Forex broker firms was compiled from the global listing of brokers provided at w**ww.forex-brokers-list.com**. The website includes a moderated listing of Forex brokers. The site guarantees that listed companies provided accurate information about their companies and their company's services, at the time data were entered into the listing. Brokers in other nations can also be found at the website.

Company title:	A. B. Watley FX, Inc.
Services:	Forex, Futures, Stocks, Options, Managed Funds, News & Analysis, Education
Languages:	Chinese (simplified), Danish, English, French, German, Greek, Hebrew, Irish, Italian, Japanese, Korean, Portuguese, Russian, Scottish, Spanish, Swedish, Turkish
Trading platform:	Flash Forex
Commissions on Forex:	no
Bid/Ask spread on Major currencies:	3-5 pips
Maximum Leverage:	100:1
Minimal Deposit Size:	$2,000 $500 (Mini account)
Free Demo Account:	yes
Mini Forex Trading:	yes
Contact info	
Address:	50 Broad Street Suite 1614
City:	New York, NY
Country:	U.S.
Telephone number:	1-888-733-9000

Company URL:	www.abwatley.com

Company title:	ApexForex.com
Address:	111 West Jackson BL Suite 2010
City:	Chicago, IL
Country:	U.S. & Canada
Zip code:	60604
Telephone number:	800-634-9466
Telephone number:	312-373-6251
Company URL:	www.apexforex.com
Services:	Forex, Futures, Options, Managed Funds, News & Analysis, Education
Languages:	English
Trading platform:	Global Trading System
Commissions on Forex:	no
Bid/Ask spread on Major currencies:	3 pips
Minimal Transaction Size:	1,000 USD
Minimal Deposit Size:	500 USD
Free Demo Account:	yes
Mini Forex Trading:	yes

Company title:	Capital Market Services, LLC. CMS Forex
Services:	CMS offers trading using the VT Trader platform where clients can execute orders automatically based on their own trading systems with FX AutoPilot. CMS features exclusive daily, weekly, and monthly commentary by world renowned Forex analyst Hans Nilsson.
Languages:	English, Spanish, German, French, Italian, Portuguese, Chinese, Japanese, Korean, Arabic, Russian, Polish, Taiwanese, Mandarin, Cantonese
Trading platform:	Visual Trading (VT Trader)
Commissions on Forex:	no

Bid/Ask spread on Major currencies:	3-4 pips
Maximum Leverage:	400:1
Minimal Deposit Size:	200 USD
Free Demo Account:	yes
Mini Forex Trading:	yes
Address:	Empire State Building 350 5th Avenue Suite 6400 New York, NY 10118
Country:	USA
Telephone number:	212-563-2100
Fax number:	212-563-4994
E-mail:	customerservice@cmsfx.com
Company URL:	www.cmsfx.com

Company title:	Currency Trading USA
Address:	Subsidiary of GAIN Capital (www.gain-capital.com)
City:	Miami, Fl
Country:	USA & Canada
Zip code:	33145
Telephone number:	877-424-6227
Telephone number:	908-731-0700 (Outside of the U.S.)
Fax number:	786-735-1658
Company URL:	www.currencytradingusa.com
Services:	Forex, Managed Funds, Education
Languages:	English, Spanish
Trading platform:	
Commissions on Forex:	no
Bid/Ask spread on Major currencies:	4-5 pips
Minimal Transaction Size:	10,000 USD
Minimal Deposit Size:	250 USD
Free Demo Account:	yes
Mini Forex Trading:	yes

Company title:	Forex Day Trading
Address:	
City:	Miami, FL
Country:	U.S. & Canada
Zip code:	33145
Telephone number:	877-424-6227
Telephone number:	908-731-0700 (Outside of the U.S.)
Fax number:	786-735-1658
Company URL:	www.forex-day-trading.com/index.htm
Services:	Forex, Managed Funds, Education
Languages:	English, Spanish
Trading platform:	
Commissions on Forex:	no
Bid/Ask spread on Major currencies:	4-5 pips
Minimal Transaction Size:	10,000 USD
Minimal Deposit Size:	250 USD
Free Demo Account:	yes
Mini Forex Trading:	yes

Company title:	FXDirectDealer
Address:	75 Park Place, 4th Floor
City:	New York, NY
Zip code:	10007
Country:	USA
Toll-free number:	1-866-FOR-FXDD (367-3933)
Main Telephone number:	1-212-791-FXDD (3933)
Fax number:	1-212-937-3845
E-mail:	sales@fxdd.com
Company URL:	www.fxdd.com
Services:	Forex
Languages:	English, Chinese Simple, Korean
Trading platform:	FXDD Trader, MetaTrader
Commissions on Forex:	no
Bid/Ask spread on Major currencies:	3-5 pips

Quoted Currencies:	19 currency pairs EUR/USD, USD/JPY, GBP/USD, USD/CHF, EUR/JPY, EUR/GBP, GBP/JPY, EUR/CHF, USD/CAD, AUD/USD, CHF/JPY, GBP/CHF, EUR/AUD, EUR/CAD, AUD/CAD, AUD/JPY, AUD/NZD, NZD/USD, USD/MXN.
Maximum Leverage:	100:1 for a regular account 200:1 for a mini account
Mini Forex Trading:	yes
Free Demo Account:	yes

Company title:	Forex.com
Address:	44 Wall Street
City:	New York, NY
Country:	U.S. & Canada
Zip code:	10005
Telephone number:	877-FOREXGO (367-3946)
Telephone number:	1-908-731-0750
Company URL:	www.forex.com
Services:	Forex
Languages:	Chinese (simplified), Chinese (traditional), English
Trading platform:	
Commissions on Forex:	yes
Bid/Ask spread on Major currencies:	4-5 pips
Minimal Transaction Size:	10 USD
Minimal Deposit Size:	250 USD
Free Demo Account:	yes
Mini Forex Trading:	yes

Company title:	FX Solutions
Address:	1 Route 17 South Suite 260
City:	Saddle River, NJ
Country:	U.S. & Canada
Zip code:	07458

Telephone number:	1-201-345-2211
E-mail:	See website
Company URL:	www.fxsolutions.com
Services:	Forex, Managed Funds
Languages:	English, Chinese (simplified), Chinese (traditional)
Trading platform:	Global Trading System
Commissions on Forex:	no
Bid/Ask spread on Major currencies:	3-4 pips
Minimal Transaction Size:	10 USD
Minimal Deposit Size:	300 USD
Free Demo Account:	yes
Mini Forex Trading:	yes

Company title:	Global Forex LLC
Address:	PO Box 6263
City:	North Logan, UT
Country:	U.S. & Canada
Zip code:	84341
Telephone number:	435-563-0057
Company URL:	www.forexonline.com
Services:	Forex
Languages:	Russian, English, Spanish, Chinese (simplified), Japanese, Armenian, French, Korean, Romanian
Trading platform:	
Commissions on Forex:	no
Bid/Ask spread on Major currencies:	4-5 pips
Minimal Transaction Size:	500 USD
Minimal Deposit Size:	2,000 USD
Free Demo Account:	yes
Mini Forex Trading:	yes

Company title:	Goldberg Forex Group
Address:	2021 Tyler St. Suite 210
City:	Hollywood, Fl
Country:	U.S. & Canada
Zip code:	33020
Telephone number:	305-947-9639
Company URL:	www.goldbergForex.com
Services:	Forex
Languages:	Chinese (simplified), English, Spanish
Trading platform:	
Commissions on Forex:	yes
Bid/Ask spread on Major currencies:	5-6 pips
Minimal Transaction Size:	10,000 USD
Minimal Deposit Size:	250 USD
Free Demo Account:	yes
Mini Forex Trading:	yes

Company title:	MVP Financial, LLC
Address:	99 John Street, #223
City:	New York, NY
Country:	U.S. & Canada
Zip code:	10038
Telephone number:	212-962-2100
Telephone number:	877-962-2100
Fax number:	212.962.3333
Company URL:	www.mvpglobalforex.com
Services:	Forex, Futures, Managed Funds, Education
Languages:	English, Chinese (simplified), Chinese (traditional)
Trading platform:	Global Trading System, J-Trader, Global Trading System (GTS)
Commissions on Forex:	no
Bid/Ask spread on Major currencies:	3-4 pips
Minimal Transaction Size:	1,000 USD

Minimal Deposit Size:	500 USD
Free Demo Account:	yes
Mini Forex Trading:	yes

Company title:	PFGBEST
Services:	Forex, Managed Forex Accounts, Futures, Options, Managed Funds, News & Analysis, Education
Languages:	English
Trading platform:	PFG MT4, allowing clients to build and execute their trading strategies on exclusive pricing. PFG Currenex institutional platform, now offered to margined investors. BEST Direct offering futures and forex over a single platform. BEST Direct FX Platinum, a complete spot platform with limited online options.
Commissions on Forex:	Yes
Bid/Ask spread on Major currencies:	
Maximum Leverage:	
Free Demo Account:	Yes
Mini Forex Trading:	Yes
Address:	One Peregrine Way Cedar Falls, IA 50613
Country:	USA
Toll Free:	1-800-361-6855 (within North America)
Int'l:	+01-312-212-3920
E-mail:	CustomerService@PFGBEST.com
Company URL:	www.pfgbest.com

Appendix E

Central Banks

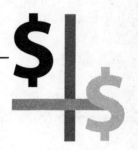

Albania: Banka e Shqipërisë
www.bankofalbania.org

Algeria: Banque d'Algerie
www.bank-of-algeria.dz

Argentina: Banco Central de la
República Argentina
www.bcra.gov.ar

Armenia: Central Bank of
Armenia
www.cba.am

Aruba: Centrale Bank van Aruba
www.cbaruba.org

Australia: Reserve Bank of
Australia
www.rba.gov.au

Austria: Oesterreichische
Nationalbank
www.oenb.at

Bahrain: Bahrain Monetary
Agency
www.bma.gov.bh

Barbados: Central Bank of
Barbados
www.centralbank.org.bb

Belgium: National Bank of
Belgium
www.bnb.be

Bermuda: Bermuda Monetary
Authority
www.bma.bm

Bolivia: Banco Central de Bolivia
www.bcb.gob.bo

Bosnia and Herzegovina:
Centralna Banka Bosne i
Hercegovine
www.cbbh.ba/

Botswana: Bank of Botswana
www.bankofbotswana.bw

Brazil: Banco Central do Brasil
www.bcb.gov.br

Bulgaria: Bulgarska Narodna Banka
www.bnb.bg

Canada: Bank of Canada
www.bankofcanada.ca/

Cape Verde: Banco de Cabo Verde
www.bcv.cv

Cayman Islands: Cayman Islands Monetary Authority
www.cimoney.com.ky

Chile: Banco Central de Chile
www.bcentral.cl

China: Zhongguo Renmin Yinhang
www.pbc.gov.cn

Colombia: Banco de la República de Colombia
www.banrep.gov.co

Costa Rica: Banco Central de Costa Rica
www.bccr.fi.cr

Croatia: Hrvatska Narodna Banka
www.hnb.hr

Cyprus: Central Bank of Cyprus
www.centralbank.gov.cy

Czech Republic: Ceska Národní Banka
www.cnb.cz

Denmark: Danmarks Nationalbank
www.nationalbanken.dk

Djibouti: Banque Nationale Djibouti
www.banque-centrale.dj

Dominican Republic: Banco Central de la República Dominicana
www.bancentral.gov.do

Eastern Caribbean: Eastern Caribbean Central Bank
www.eccb-centralbank.org

Ecuador: Banco Central del Ecuador
www.bce.fin.ec

El Salvador: Banco Central de Reserva de El Salvador
www.bcr.gob.sv

Estonia: Eesti Pank
www.bankofestonia.info/ frontpage/en

European Central Bank
www.ecb.int/home/html/index. en.html

Faroe Islands: Landsbanki Føroya
www.landsbank.fo

Fiji: Reserve Bank of Fiji
www.reservebank.gov.fj

Finland: Suomen Pankki
www.bof.fi

France: Banque de France
www.banque-france.fr

Georgia: National Bank of
Georgia
www.nbg.gov.ge

Germany: Deutsche Bundesbank
www.bundesbank.de

Greece: Bank of Greece
www.bankofgreece.gr

Guatemala: Banco de Guatemala
www.banguat.gob.gt

Guyana: Bank of Guyana
www.bankofguyana.org.gy

Haiti: Banque de la République
d'Haïti
www.brh.net

Honduras: Banco Central de
Honduras
www.bch.hn

Hong Kong: Hong Kong
Monetary Authority
www.info.gov.hk/hkma

Hungary: Magyar Nemzeti Bank
www.mnb.hu

Iceland: Seðlabanki Íslands
www.sedlabanki.is

India: Reserve Bank of India
www.rbi.org.in

Indonesia: Bank Sentral Republik
Indonesia
www.bi.go.id/web/id/

Iran: Central Bank of the Islamic
Republic of Iran
www.cbi.ir

Ireland: Central Bank of Ireland
www.centralbank.ie

Israel: Bank of Israel
www.bankisrael.gov.il

Italy: Banca d'Italia
www.bancaditalia.it

Jamaica: Bank of Jamaica
www.boj.org.jm

Japan: Bank of Japan
www.boj.or.jp

Jordan: Central Bank of Jordan
www.cbj.gov.jo

Kazakhstan: Kazakstan Ulttyk
Banki
www.nationalbank.kz

Kenya: Central Bank of Kenya
www.centralbank.go.ke

Korea, South: Bank of Korea
www.bok.or.kr

Kuwait: Central Bank of Kuwait
www.cbk.gov.kw

Latvia: Latvijas Banka
www.bank.lv

Lebanon: Banque Du Liban
www.bdl.gov.lb

Lesotho: Central Bank of Lesotho
www.centralbank.org.ls

Lithuania: Lietuvos Bankas
www.lbank.lt

Luxembourg: Banque Centrale de
Luxembourg
www.bcl.lu

Macau: Monetary Authority of
Macau
www.amcm.gov.mo

Macedonia, Former Yugoslav
Republic of: National Bank of the
Republic of Macedonia
www.nbrm.gov.mk

Malawi: Reserve Bank of Malawi
www.rbm.mw

Malaysia: Bank Negara Malaysia
www.bnm.gov.my

Malta: Central Bank of Malta
www.centralbankmalta.com

Mauritius: Bank of Mauritius
http://bom.intnet.mu

Mexico: Banco de México
www.banxico.org.mx

Moldova: National Bank of
Moldova
www.bnm.org/en/home

Mozambique: Banco de
Moçambique
www.bancomoc.mz

Namibia: Bank of Namibia
www.bon.com.na

Nepal: Nepal Rastra Bank
www.nrb.org.np

Netherlands Antilles: Bank van de
Nederlandse Antillen
www.centralbank.an

Netherlands: Nederlandsche Bank
www.dnb.nl

New Zealand: Reserve Bank of New Zealand
www.rbnz.govt.nz

Nicaragua: Banco Central de Nicaragua
www.bcn.gob.ni

Norway: Norges Bank
www.norges-bank.no

Oman: Central Bank Of Oman
www.cbo-oman.org

Pakistan: State Bank of Pakistan
www.sbp.org.pk

Palestinian Authority: Palestinian Monetary Authority
www.pma.ps

Paraguay: Banco Central del Paraguay
www.bcp.gov.py

Peru: Banco Central de Reserva del Peru
www.bcrp.gob.pe

Philippines: Bangko Sentral ng Pilipinas
www.bsp.gov.ph

Poland: Narodowy Bank Polski
www.nbp.pl

Portugal: Banco de Portugal
www.bportugal.pt

Qatar: Qatar Central Bank
www.qcb.gov.qa

Romania: National Bank of Romania
www.bnro.ro

Russia: Bank of Russia
www.cbr.ru

San Marino: Istituto di Credito Sammarinese
www.bcsm.sm

Saudi Arabia: Saudi Arabian Monetary Agency
www.sama.gov.sa

Singapore: Monetary Authority of Singapore
www.mas.gov.sg

Slovakia: Národná Banka Slovenska
www.nbs.sk

Slovenia: Banka Slovenije
www.bsi.si

South Africa: South African Reserve Bank
www.resbank.co.za

Spain: Banco de España
www.bde.es

Swaziland: Central Bank of
Swaziland
www.centralbank.org.sz

Sweden: Sveriges Riksbank
www.riksbank.se

Switzerland: Schweiserische
Nationalbank
www.snb.ch

Taiwan: Central Bank of China
www.cbc.gov.tw

Tanzania: Bank of Tanzania
www.bot-tz.org

Thailand: Bank of Thailand
www.bot.or.th

Trinidad and Tobago: Central
Bank of Trinidad and Tobago
www.central-bank.org.tt

Tunisia: Banque Centrale de
Tunisie
www.bct.gov.tn

Turkey: Türkiye Cumhuriyet
Merkez Bankasi
www.tcmb.gov.tr

Uganda: Bank of Uganda
www.bou.or.ug

Ukraine: National Bank of
Ukraine
www.bank.gov.ua

United Arab Emirates: Central
Bank of the United Arab Emirates
www.cbuae.gov.ae

United Kingdom: Bank of
England
www.bankofengland.co.uk

United States Federal Reserve
System
**www.federalreserve.gov/
otherfrb.htm**

Uruguay: Banco Central del
Uruguay
www.bcu.gub.uy

Venezuela: Banco Central de
Venezuela
www.bcv.org.ve

West Africa: Banque Centrale des
Etats de l'Afrique de l'Ouest
www.bceao.int

Yemen: Central Bank of Yemen
www.centralbank.gov.ye

Zimbabwe: Reserve Bank of
Zimbabwe
www.rbz.co.zw

Appendix F

Internet Resources

The Internet is flooded with news and information that can help you anticipate market movements, educate yourself, and expand your trading strategies. Hundreds of forex sites offer trading tools and advice. Below are some helpful resources:

Market Data and Fundamentals

Actionforex.com (**www.actionforex.com/fundamental-analysis/weekly-forex-fundamentals/emu-economic-indicators-preview-20091109100165**): Weekly forex fundamentals.

FXStreet.com (**www.fxstreet.com/fundamental/economic-calendar**): A calendar of economic indicators.

International Monetary Fund (IMF) (**www.imf.org**): Information and statistics.

New York Federal Reserve (**www.newyorkfed.org/research/global_economy/globalindicators.html**): Charts of global economic indicators.

The Euro (**www.nationalbanken.dk/DNUK/Euro.nsf/side/Introduc-tion_to_the_euro!OpenDocument**): Information from the National Bank of Denmark.

Times Online (**http://business.timesonline.co.uk/tol/business/mar-kets/article6896703.ece**): Market data and a calendar of scheduled eco-nomic news releases.

Regulatory Agencies

Bank for International Settlements (BIS) (**www.bis.org**): An interna-tional organization that promotes international financial and monetary cooperation. The BIS serves as a bank for the central banks. The BIS is headquartered in Switzerland with two offices in Hong Kong and Mexico City.

Commodity Futures Trading Commission (CFTC) (**www.cftc.gov**): A U.S. government body that monitors the activities of the NFA.

Financial Service Authority of the United Kingdom (FSA) (**www.fsa.gov.uk**): A non-government, independent organization that has regu-lated the financial services industry in the United Kingdom since 2000.

Investment Industry Regulatory Organization of Canada (IRROC) (**www.iiroc.ca/English/Pages/home.aspx**): A national self-regulatory member organization for the Canadian securities industry.

National Futures Association (NFA) (**www.nfa.futures.org**): A U.S.-based self-regulated organization that provides regulatory programs, market integrity, and oversight to industry-wide futures and forex mar-kets.

U.S. Securities and Exchange Commission (SEC) (**www.sec.gov**): A U.S. government body that exists to protect investors; maintain fair, efficient, orderly markets; and to facilitate the formation of capital to sustain economic growth.

Securities and Futures Commission of Hong Kong (SFC) (**www.sfc.hk/sfc/html/EN**): An independent non-governmental statutory body that has jurisdiction over securities and futures markets in the city of Hong Kong.

Swiss Federal Banking Commission (SFBC) (**www.finma.ch/archiv/ebk/e/index.html**): An independent administrative authority of the Confederation that supervises particular areas of the Switzerland financial sector.

Articles and Education

"Forex Secrets: Trading The US Dollar (USD)" by Robin Lofton, November 23, 2009. (**http://currencies.suite101.com/article.cfm/forex_secrets**)

Investopedia.com (**www.investopedia.com/articles/forex/?viewed=1**): A ValueClick, Inc. website offering numerous articles on forex topics.

FX Words (**www.fxwords.com**): Forex glossary.

Finding a Broker

Brokersmatrix.com (**www.brokersmatrix.com**): A site that allows you to select and compare brokers.

BASIC (**www.nfa.futures.org/basicnet**): This is the CFTC database of all registered Futures Commission Merchants (FCMs) and Introducing Brokers (IBs). You can also find information on companies that have been disciplined for ethical and financial violations.

Forex Hoster (**www.forexhoster.com**): Virtual Private Server (VPS) provider.

Forex VPS (**www.forexvps.com**): VPS provider.

Price Charts and Technical Indicators

DailyFX.com (**www.dailyfx.com/charts**): Free pricing charts.

ForexPros.com (**www.forexpros.com/charts**): Free pricing charts.

Currency Trading USA (**www.currencytradingusa.com/fibonacci. htm**): Fibonacci retracements.

Appendix G

Economic Indicators for Major Trading Markets

Major Trading Markets

	U.S. (dollar)	Europe (euro)	Japan (yen)	Great Britain (pound)	Switzerland (franc)	Canada (dollar)	Australia (dollar)	New Zealand (dollar)
Type of Economy	Service-Oriented	Trade, Capital Flow, & Service Oriented	Manu-facture-Oriented	Service-Oriented	Capital and Trade Flows	Service-Oriented	Service-Oriented	Trade-Oriented
Central Bank	Federal Reserve Bank (Fed)	European Central Bank (ECB)	Bank of Japan (BOJ)	Bank of England (BOE)	Swiss National Bank (SNB)	Bank of Canada (BOC)	Reserve Bank of Australia (RBA)	Reserve Bank of New Zealand (RBNZ)
Central Bank Interest	Federal Funds Target Rate	ECB Minimum Bid Rate		Bank Repo Rate	Swiss LIBOR rate	Bank Rate	Cash Rate	
IMF estimate of GDP	$12.2 trillion	$12.4 trillion	$3.9 trillion	$1.8 trillion	$236.9 million	$1.1 trillion	$630.1 million	$101.6 million
Inflation Target	Federal Funds Target Rate	0% to 2% of the HICP	0	2.5% growth in RPI-X	Swiss Libor Rate	1%-3%	2%-3% of CPI	1.5% of CPI

Important Indicators

	U.S. (dollar)		Europe (euro)	Japan (yen)	Great Britain (pound)	Switzer-land (franc)	Canada (dollar)	Austra-lia (dollar)	New Zealand (dollar)
Gross Domestic Product Ranking	1st		Unranked	3rd	6th	39th	11th	17th	58th
Producer Price Index	PPI	X					X	X	X
Consumer Price Index	CPI	X	HICP			X	X	X	X
Industrial Production	IP	X	X	X	X	Pro-duc-tion Index			
Institute Supply Manage-ment Index	ISM index	X							
Durable Goods and Services		X						Bal-ance of Goods and Ser-vices	Bal-ance of Goods and Ser-vices
Consumer Confidence		X							
Employ-ment Cost Index	ECI	X	X	Data, not an Index	Data, not an Index		Data, not an Index		
Retail Sales	RSI	X			Retail Price Index	X			
Housing Starts		X			X				
Balance of Internation-al Trade		X					X		

Balance of Payments		X		X		X			
Private Consumption		X					Consumer Consumption	X	X
Treasury International Capital Flow	TIC flow								
Information and Forschung Survey	IFS		X						
Tankan Survey				X					
Budget Deficit			X						
Purchasing Manager's Index	PMI				X				
KoF						X			

Bibliography

All websites accessed February 16, 2010.

Archer, Michael D. Getting started in currency trading winning in today's hottest marketplace. Getting started in …. Hoboken, N.J.: John Wiley & Sons. 2008.

Bank for International Settlements. Triennial Central Bank Survey, December 2007: Foreign exchange and derivatives market activity in 2007. 2007. (**www.bis.org/publ/rpfxf07t.pdf?noframes=1**)

Brown, Kedrick F. Trend trading: timing market tides. Wiley Trading. Hoboken, N.J.: J. Wiley & Sons. 2006.

Central Intelligence Agency. The World Fact Book. (Updated bi-weekly) (**www.cia.gov/library/publications/the-world-factbook/index.html**).

Chen, James. Essentials of foreign exchange trading. Hoboken, N.J.: John Wiley. 2009.

Economic Research Service, U.S. Department of Agriculture. Real Historical Gross Domestic Product (GDP) and Growth Rates of GDP. November 2009. (**www.ers.usda.gov/Data/Macroeconomics**).

Foreign Exchange Committee. Overview of the OTC Foreign Exchange Market: 2009. November 9, 2009. (**www.newyorkfed.org/fxc/news/2009/overview_nov_2009.pdf**).

"Forex Capital Markets." Wealthyaffiliatecoach.com. January 10, 2010. (**http://wealthyaffiliatecoach.com/forex-capital-markets-10**).

Forex-demo-account.org. "Forex Trading Online As a Part of Investment Portfolio." August 8, 2009. (**http://forex-demo-account. org/forex-trading-online-as-a-part-of-investment-portfolio**).

Galant, Mark, and Brian Dolan. Currency trading for dummies. Hoboken, N.J.: Wiley. 2007.

Jagerson, John. **"Currency ETFs Simplify Forex Trades."** Investopedia.com (**www.investopedia.com/articles/forex/07/currency-ETFs.asp**).

Laïdi, Ashraf. Currency trading and intermarket analysis: how to profit from the shifting currents in global markets. Hoboken, N.J.: John Wiley & Sons. 2009.

Lee, Richard. "Ichimoku Cloud Filters Information Storm." Investo-pedia.com. (**www.investopedia.com/articles/forex/06/ichimoku.asp**).

Lien, Kathy. Day trading the currency market: technical and fundamental strategies to profit from market swings. Wiley trading series. Hoboken, N.J.: John Wiley & Sons. 2006.

Oxford Analytica. "The Greece Dilemma." Forbes.com. January 15, 2010, (**www.forbes.com/2010/01/14/greece-eu-bonds-business-oxford-analytica.html**).

Pierron, Axel. Electronic Platforms in Foreign Exchange Trading. Celent. 2007 (**www.e-forex.net/Files/surveyreportsPDFs/Celent%20FX%20report.pdf**).

Rosenstreich, Peter. Forex revolution: an insider's guide to the real world of foreign exchange trading. Indianapolis, IN: Financial Times Prentice Hall Books. 2005.

Schlossberg, Boris. Technical analysis of the currency market: classic techniques for profiting from market swings and trader sentiment. Wiley trading. Hoboken, N.J.: John Wiley. 2006.

Taxiarchos, John. "How Forex and Stock Trading Differ." Trading-Markets.com. December 18, 2008. (**www.tradingmarkets.com/.site/forex/how_to/articles/The-Forex-Market-vs-The-Stock-Market-79602.cfm**).

Tilkin, Gary, and Lita Epstein. The complete idiot's guide to foreign currency trading. Indianapolis, IN: Alpha Books. 2007.

U.S. Energy Information Administration. Independent Statistics and Analysis. (**http://tonto.eia.doe.gov/country/index.cfm**).

Van Bergen, Jason. "A Primer On The Forex Market." Investopedia. com. (**www.investopedia.com/articles/trading/03/091703.asp**).

World Bank. Gross domestic product 2008. October 2009. (**http:// siteresources.worldbank.org/DATASTATISTICS/Resources/ GDP.pdf**).

Authors' Biographies

Martha Maeda is an economic historian and writes on politics, ethics, and modern philosophy. After graduating from Northwestern University, she lived and worked in Australia, Japan, Latin America, and several African countries before settling in the United States. She has a special interest in microeconomics and the effects of globalization on the lives and businesses of people all over the world. She is the author of several books on personal finance including *The Complete Guide to Investing in Exchange Traded Funds*, *The Complete Guide to Investing in Bonds and Bond Funds*, *How to Wipe Out Your Student Loans and be Debt Free Fast*, *The Complete Guide to IRAs and IRA Investing*, and *The Complete Guide to Spotting Accounting Fraud and Cover-ups*.

Jamaine Burrell is a writer who lives in Baltimore. Her many talents have led to authorship of this book as well as other books with the Atlantic Publishing Group including *The Rental Propery Manager's Toolbox: A Complete Guide Including Pre-Written Forms, Agreements, Letters, and Legal Notices — With Companion CD-ROM* and *How to Repair Your Credit Score Now: Simple No Cost Methods You Can Put to Use Today.*

Index